# MEMORIAL TO A MARRIAGE

# MEMORIAL
# TO A MARRIAGE

*An Album on the Saint-Gaudens Memorial*

*in Rock Creek Cemetery*

*Commissioned by Henry Adams in Honor of*

*His Wife, Marian Hooper Adams*

## ESSAY BY LINCOLN KIRSTEIN
## PHOTOGRAPH ALBUM BY
## JERRY L. THOMPSON

*Additional photographs by Marian Hooper Adams*

THE METROPOLITAN MUSEUM OF ART

DISTRIBUTED BY HARRY N. ABRAMS, INC.

*New York*

This book has been published with funds provided by
The William Cullen Bryant Fellows of The American Wing.

*Library of Congress Cataloging-in-Publication Data*

Kirstein, Lincoln, 1907–
Memorial to a marriage: an album on the Saint-Gaudens Memorial in
Rock Creek Cemetery commissioned by Henry Adams in honor of his wife,
Marian Hooper Adams / essay by Lincoln Kirstein; photograph album
by Jerry L. Thompson; additional photographs by Marian Hooper Adams.
p.    cm.        Bibliography: p.
ISBN 0–87099–524–3      ISBN 0–8109–3600–3 (Abrams)
1. Adams, Marian, 1843–1885.    2. Adams, Marian, 1843–1885—Monuments.
3. Adams, Henry, 1838–1918.    4. Saint-Gaudens, Augustus, 1848–1907.
5. United States—Biography.    6. Adams Memorial (Washington, D.C.)—Pictorial works.
7. Washington (D.C.)—Buildings, structures, etc.—Pictorial works.
I. Thompson, Jerry L.    II. Adams, Marian, 1843–1885.    III. Title.
CT275.A34K57    1989        973.5'092—dc20        [B]
89–9214    CIP

FRONTISPIECE:
Augustus Saint-Gaudens. *The Adams Memorial*, 1886–91.
Bronze figure cast 1969, over life-size (detail). Washington, D.C.,
National Museum of American Art, Smithsonian Institution, 1970.11

# FOREWORD

Lincoln Kirstein, perhaps best known as cofounder and president of the School of American Ballet and cofounder and general director of the New York City Ballet, is in addition a patron of the arts, an eclectic collector, an activist pro bono publico, a poet, a novelist, and a belletrist of unceasing productivity. He is also an inveterate museum-goer. His election in 1967 as a Benefactor of the Metropolitan Museum marked a long and valued association that continues to this day. Included among the gifts he has made to the Museum are sculptural objects, vast quantities of books whose titles reflect his boundless intellectual curiosity, and a multitude of photographs and prints, the latter revealed in 1986 by the Metropolitan's *Impressions of a New Civilization: The Lincoln Kirstein Collection of Japanese Prints (1860–1912)*, an exhibition of works he had prized for their charm thirty years before his critical judgment was vindicated. Mr. Kirstein has displayed his connoisseurship of American sculpture in writings on such divergent stylists as William Rimmer, Gaston Lachaise, and Elie Nadelman. The cast of Augustus Saint-Gaudens's *Diana* that he presented to the Department of American Paintings and Sculpture in 1985 is a manifestation of his admiration for that most technically skilled of all American sculptors. It is therefore highly appropriate for the Museum to publish *Memorial to a Marriage*, which contains Mr. Kirstein's essay on Saint-Gaudens's Adams Memorial, not only for the singular comprehension he brings to the subject but also as an expression of the affection and esteem in which we hold him.

Jerry L. Thompson, the artist-photographer whose album of studies of the memorial is a pendant to the essay, has made sculpture his specialty since the early nineteen-seventies. In 1983, he became affiliated with the Metropolitan in an undertaking to commit to film the American Wing's some four hundred pieces of sculpture, a project he has all but completed. He became particularly absorbed in the Adams Memorial through his contribution to the monograph on Augustus Saint-Gaudens that the Museum issued in 1985 to accompany an exhibition of the sculptor's work. The collaboration between the two authors began in 1984, when Mr. Thompson began to photograph Mr. Kirstein's collection. *Memorial to a Marriage* is the result of their common interest in the problems inherent in the visual recording of three-dimensional objects and, of equal importance, in the many facets of the monument itself.

The publication of this volume has been underwritten in full by The William Cullen Bryant Fellows of The American Wing. As always, the Museum is indebted to the Bryant Fellows for their generosity in sponsoring books devoted to the American arts.

PHILIPPE DE MONTEBELLO
*Director*
*The Metropolitan Museum of Art*

IN MEMORIAM: JOSEPH DUELL

# ACKNOWLEDGMENTS

IN 1919, my sister, Mina Curtiss, wrote her master's thesis for Radcliffe on the previously uncollected articles of Henry Adams in the *North American Review*. I was reared in Boston. At Harvard, beginning in 1926, I was lucky enough to know members of the Lowell, Cabot, Sturgis, and Adams families. In 1928, Mrs. Winthrop Chanler, a close friend of Adams's, showed me copies of his poem "Prayer to the Dynamo" and two of his books, *The Education of Henry Adams* and *Mont-Saint-Michel and Chartres*, each bearing a handwritten dedication ("To my sister in Christ"), which he had sent to her. All these factors contributed to my lifelong interest in that key educator of himself and others.

This essay on the Adams Memorial depended on no original research. To have written it without reference to the several excellent books listed in the Bibliography would have been impossible.

Professor Edward Mendelson, of Columbia University, read my manuscript and made many corrections and suggestions. His assistance always benefits anything I write. My heaviest obligation in preparing this book is to Lewis Sharp, who instigated it, and to Mary-Alice Rogers, who made sound and sense of it.

LINCOLN KIRSTEIN
*New York, 1989*

# THE ADAMS MEMORIAL

MEMORIAL TO A MARRIAGE

# I.

AN ENIGMA SEEMINGLY IMPENETRABLE for nearly a century is rarely illuminated to near transparency, but here, with time's passage and after the release of relevant documents, secrets initially shrouded in earnest ambiguity both philosophical and aesthetic and eventually cast in memorial bronze have been in great part disclosed. In the process have also been revealed aspects of the monument that raised it to a level approaching a national touchstone. If one searches for a single piece of glyptic art incorporating a key metaphysical crux of the late nineteenth century, it is to be found in this androgynous presence masterfully modeled by Augustus Saint-Gaudens. In its bearing on art and behavior, its figuration involves facets of an alien cosmology opposed, or alternative, to the traditional descent of New England's transcendentalism. Here also enshrined are archetypes of old American society and culture, two self-proclaimed failures who have come to be canonized through heroism implicit in private marriage and public morality.

As far as those most affected were concerned, Marian Hooper Adams's suicide was intended to remain forever unrecognized as a matter too abysmal for reason or remembrance. After thirteen years of married life happier than many, she took poison. It was long assumed that her husband then destroyed every letter, every photograph of her or by her then in his possession. However, after Adams's death in 1918 his executor turned over to the eldest of Mrs. Adams's five nieces a half-dozen packets of her letters, arranged in chronological order and marked in Adams's hand. No letter survived from the first two or the last two winters in Washington, perhaps the happiest and the saddest of their life together. In the autobiography he had come to write some twenty years later, her name is not mentioned.

The tragedy's shock struck a wide network of relatives and friends who would vividly recall it after years of loyal silence. Two full studies of Mrs. Adams's life and death exist. While no one ever may know the whole tale, there is enough to suggest plainly how despair was prompted and grew; how one individual's fragile mortality became transfigured into deathless sculpture.

After rumor dissipated, having fused into legend, objective testimony remained. The hooded figure in weather-streaked bronze miles from downtown Washington declares in its holly-hedged isolation an otherworldliness that is less icon than embodiment. Impersonal and sexless it sits, its tireless level aspect serenely unquestioning, dispassionate in all-acceptance. Minerals from which it is cast, carved stone that frames it scorn the scars of rain and frost that only heighten its immutable finality. Yet beneath the aura of oracular myth lie subtrata of steady, permanent reference. The spectral presences of three spirits continue to testify, not only as mute, masked, or passionate players but also as active representatives of the large considerations that sign their epoch.

## II.

Its cemetery location demands attention to this statue's attachment to last things. Saint-Gaudens, its sculptor, despite Franco-Irish roots, was not a communicant of the Roman Church but a worshiper in the religion of classical art. Both Adamses were high Boston Brahmins, affluent heirs of post-Emersonian transcendentalism. They thought and behaved in protestant flight from the Calvinist strictures of an exalted, seventeenth-century puritanical ancestry that continued to agonize its nineteenth-century heirs. Their course was determined by the Sage of Concord's loose doctrine of free will, self-determination, and personal distinction in aristocratic achievement, which was ultimately solipsism, holding the individual self above all else. Yet each was a pilgrim on a path, striving to make sense and order of what was granted from caste, talent, and the day's chances. Both were absorbed in a preoccupation with history. Historicism was Henry Adams's quasi-scientific substitute for the doctrinal Catholicism he felt constrained to discount, although its man-made artifacts, its cathedral portals and windows, were magnets to his genuine idolatry.

Saint-Gaudens the artist was freed from many or most uncertainties by unquestionable genius that could be constantly corroborated by accomplishment. But for the Adams pair, caught compulsively in their strivings toward intellectual, ethical, and aesthetic perfection, the strain built to a mutual undoing. Marian Adams abandoned her struggle before she could have counted it half-engaged. Her husband judged himself a consummate failure, yet as political journalist, historian, novelist, poet, and thinker, he ranks with the leaders of his time. His elaborate apologia was an echo of his inverted pride. Although his brilliant publications compile a rich bibliography, he boasted that his books were unread; his talents, the lax promptings of an amateur. The Socratic pose of questioning ignorance he assumed would always mean that in comparison with everyone else he was the less unknowing. Even his best friends admitted that he wanted the world thrust upon him on a silver platter. Van Wyck Brooks, coming from the same roots, wrote: "Vanity, in short, was Henry Adams' governing motive, as one saw in the anonymity to which he resorted. If he could not have fame at once, he would not play."

40

As for his wife, today she may be classed as a protofeminist martyr to frustrations implicit in an arrested male prejudice, augmented by the ineradicable disappointment, mental and physical, of childless womanhood. She did her best to compensate by serving occasionally as her husband's research assistant or copyist, and was extraordinarily successful as a *saloneuse*, a popular political hostess in the most prestigious society. But when she turned with deep, and even desperate, interest to photography as self-expression or self-vindication, aiming at a technical proficiency not less than professional, his class prejudice at owning a working wife was to her but the final proof of her inborn inadequacy to compete with the superior male. He possessively encouraged her strivings for the personal dignity she merited by virtue of her brains, breeding, and behavior, but he denied her the individual status she prized and deserved. Marian Adams lacked that vital focus which, given prevailing attitudes, her husband may have been powerless to extend.

## III.

MARIAN STURGIS HOOPER, known as Clover from childhood, was born in 1843, a thrice-proper Bostonian. Her father, Robert William Hooper, was an eminent ophthalmologist rich enough to evade formal practice. The family was one of the most ancient and honorable clans of New England landed oligarchy — Sturgis, Cabot, Shaw, Lowell, Bancroft, all in the solid intermarried lineage of patrician liberalism. Robert Gould Shaw, colonel of the celebrated regiment of black volunteers massacred at Fort Wagner in 1863 and immortalized by Saint-Gaudens's great high relief on Boston Common, was her second cousin. Her mother died when she was five, precipitating a fervent attachment to her father that survived marriage as the virtual core of her existence.

## IV.

WHEN she was fourteen, she was enrolled in Elizabeth Agassiz's progressive classes for young girls, which not long afterward developed into an academic annex to Harvard College and in 1894 achieved official incorporation as Radcliffe. As with the offspring of many abolitionist Bostonians, pursuits of the mind were not only permitted but, within limits of gender, even encouraged. Latin, Greek, German, classical and modern literature, music, art were obligatory diversion and adornment, accompanied by daily fluctuating reports from the battlefields of Virginia and Tennessee. In motherless adolescence, one of her strongest influences was her aunt Caroline Tappan, a close follower of the transcendentalist coterie, a prolific poet, and a feminist ahead of her time. A poem of hers, titled "Disenfranchised," is a wistful statement of her views:

Standing like statues, ever in one place,
When every man a citizen shall be,
But I and all my sisters long must wait,
Enforced obedience our childish fate.

Clover Hooper was hardly a banner-bearing activist, but privately she too subscribed to women's causes, though certainly in girlhood, and well into marriage, she had no reason to feel less than free to think and act as she fancied. If she was not permitted to attend classes alongside her brother at Harvard, she was quite as well-read and informed. If she was unable to vote for Andrew Johnson or Ulysses S. Grant, it was no great deprivation. Throughout the Civil War, she served faithfully with her cousins and friends in the Sanitary Commission's female auxiliary, rolling bandages while *Vanity Fair* was read aloud to those platoons of patriotic virgins. Immediately after the grave news from Gettysburg, Dr. Hooper issued from retirement and volunteered for the field. Edward (Ned) Hooper, Clover's brother, together with Charles Francis Adams, Henry's censorious and more aggressive brother, was at Port Royal, detailed to the propaganda project of educating the blacks of the offshore Carolina islands.

Following Appomattox, Clover, with stubborn dash and ingenuity, managed to land herself in Washington in the company of other unmarried debutantes to witness two days of parading by the victorious Grand Army of the Republic. She was seated in the grandstand directly opposite President Johnson, General Grant, and General William Tecumseh Sherman. Herself an accomplished equestrienne, she was greatly impressed by the manège of Colonel George Custer (later of the Little Bighorn) as he gentled a fractious steed. With her companions she inspected the tiny room in which Abraham Lincoln died, chilled by the sight of bloody pillows on an unchanged bed. Attending the military tribunal that tried the conspirators, she observed the facial expressions of the assassins as the key to their guilt. Mrs. Surratt was veiled. She would hang with other guests of her roominghouse, though some thought that as a woman she was less culpable.

## V.

THE normal flow of Beacon Hill nuptials, interrupted by war, now resumed. Ellen Hooper, Clover's adored sister, married Ephraim Gurney, a worthy fellow who, like Emerson, forsook the pulpit. Gurney became dean of the faculty by which Charles

*Unknown photographer.*
*Tintype of Marian Hooper, 1869*

William Eliot transformed Harvard College into its new magnitude as a great university. When Clover was twenty-two, Dr. Hooper, released from the army, took her to Europe. On 16 May 1866, they dined at the American Embassy in London, where Minister Charles Francis Adams had as his private secretary his son Henry Brooks Adams, aged twenty-eight. In Henry's daybook, cramped in copperplate script at the tail of a guest list, one reads "Dr. & Miss Hooper." The encounter was perfunctory.

On 5 June 1863, young Adams, feeling guilty at staying the war out, scarless, had written his brother Charles Francis that he was bored in London and longed "to go home and take a commission in a negro regiment." That was the 54th Massachusetts Volunteer Infantry, under Colonel Robert Gould Shaw, which was massacred at Fort Wagner five weeks later. Charles Francis boasted that he'd napped through cannonades at Gettysburg and Antietam. Supercilious, begrudging, yet in early years affectionate, he told Henry he was more useful in London as his father's aide and confidant

43

than he would be as one more body in uniform. It was touch and go until three-quarters through the war whether or not Queen Victoria's government would recognize the Confederacy. Britain had forsworn slavery early in the century. Now, Manchester's mill-owners, hard-pressed by the North's naval blockade, lacked cotton to spin or sell. England's midlands starved. Because of the redoubtable skill, tact, and forbearance of Minister Adams, a frail neutrality triumphed in the face of disastrously provocative incidents that otherwise might have led to intervention first by Britain and then by other European nations. Henry would recall that he had been "private secretary in the morning, son in the afternoon and man about town in the evening." He would confess that though he was schooled at Harvard, his true education had begun in London. In England, two of his lifelong friendships were forged. The packed files of his correspondence with Charles Milnes Gaskell and Sir Robert Cunliffe are almost as important to the reconstruction of his career as is his autobiography.

Henry Adams was born in 1838. His mother's father, Peter Chardon Brooks, was the richest merchant in New England, hence the grandson would always be more than comfortably well-off. His great-grandfather was John Adams, part author of the Declaration of Independence and Washington's successor in the presidency. His grandfather was John Quincy Adams, diplomat at twenty-six, then secretary of state, finally sixth president. It was confidently expected that his father, the senior Charles Francis Adams, would also come to inhabit the White House. The expectation was almost realized. In little Henry's turn, an Irish gardener at the ancestral Quincy home said: "An' you'll be thinkin' you'll be President, too!"

Henry called his best-known book an "education." One way or another, he fulfilled the role of virtuoso instructor for the rest of his days, whether his students were Harvard collegians, his wife, his brothers, his friends, or, at the end, a mesmerized cluster of nieces and near-nieces. His oeuvre—an enormous number of books, articles, and reviews, derived from firsthand experience or from research in American history, Gothic architecture, philosophical speculation on the measure of human events and the nature of man—establishes a formidable reputation. From birth he was at home in the highest reaches of political and intellectual action. Observing as a youth in Britain the diplomatic negotiations that had preserved his country's sovereignty lent him profound insight into the manipulation of power in which ultimately, despite ambition and aptitude, he had not enough hardihood to participate. In his *Education*, he wrote of himself in 1861, at the beginning of his service to his father: "As for the private secretary . . . he was, like all Bostonians, instinctively English"; in 1866, the year of his first encounter with his wife, he described himself "dragged on one side into English dilettantism, which of all dilettantism he held the most futile; and, on the other, into American antiquarianism, which of all antiquarianism, he held the most foolish." That was, of course,

44

a less than half-true deprecation adorning considerable human experience. He was already recognized for his merits, but modesty was a stylistic affectation that gave a wry charm to his artificed writing.


## VI.

In July 1868, the Adamses, father and son, landed in Manhattan, relieved of diplomatic duties. What lay ahead? They'd been seven years away from home. Diplomacy was no longer an option without lifetime commitment. Both had already had quite enough. Henry Adams wished to become a writer. But what sort? How to proceed? In Washington, he was offered a desk in the attorney general's office. He had no legal training. The lack was crucial. However, he managed to write an extensive analysis of the current congressional scene, which the Democratic National Committee printed and circulated four years later, during the presidential campaign against Ulysses S. Grant.

In November 1868, Adams wrote to his friend Ralph Palmer, a British barrister:

> Your list of engagements shows that somehow or other the aristocracy means in both sexes to copulate according to law, both civil and canonical. This is better than to do it illegally; at least in my opinion; though hitherto I have proceeded on the latter theory. I wish someone would take the trouble to marry me out-of-hand. I've asked my mother and all my aunts to undertake the negotiation, promising to accept anyone they selected. . . . All the women acknowledge that no man is fit to choose himself a wife, and yet they all ridicule the idea of doing it for him.

Any forced or quick decision about his future was averted when he was called to Italy by his sister Louisa's illness and subsequent death. When he returned to Quincy, President Eliot of Harvard persuaded him to become an assistant professor of history. In the next seven years, with one sabbatical break, Adams taught European history from the year A.D. 989, medieval history and institutions, English constitutional history and law, American colonial and early federal history, and a graduate seminar in Anglo-Saxon law. He demanded from the outset absolute academic freedom, and won it. He had no prior experience in teaching, but he exactly suited those principles that Eliot promoted. He was a memorable instructor who numbered among his students Albert Bushnell Hart and Henry Osborn Taylor, leading professional historians of their generation, and Henry Cabot Lodge, later an influential Massachusetts senator and Woodrow Wilson's nemesis, who was awarded Harvard's first Ph.D. degree in history.

Adams also became editor of *North American Review*, a learned quarterly devoted to political reform and contemporary science. In the spring of 1872, he was offered a position on the *New York Tribune*. Given his name, erudition, and financial independ-

ence, it could have led to a career as a political pundit, but, familiar with the uses of the press and with journalists' often corrupt reaction to political pressure, he chose to remain teaching as editor and historian. There were other commanding factors. He enjoyed the comfortable life of Quincy and Harvard, and he was engaged to be married.

In a letter he wrote that year, Adams depicted himself as a social butterfly suffering from "a contemptible weakness for women's society." He blushed at the follies he was committing: "In this Arcadian society sexual passions seem to be abolished. Whether it is so or not, I can't say, but I suspect both men and women are cold, and love only with great refinement. How they ever reconcile themselves to the brutalities of marriage, I don't know."

In Boston, Clover kept house for her father with charm and efficiency, the complacent habit of her high-minded Sturgis, Shaw, Higginson, Cabot, Brooks, and Bancroft cousinage. She took long conversational walks with young Oliver Wendell Holmes, who did most of the talking. She was acquainted with the junior Henry James, then at Harvard, who admired her spirited qualities and unabashedly borrowed them for the heroines of some of his books, including *Daisy Miller*, whom Clover defended when Daisy was attacked as unfeminine by outraged readers and reviewers. His friendship would continue to the end of her life. As for Henry Adams, in the small world of patrician Boston to which he and she both belonged, they inevitably met again. They continued to see each other. Their friendship ripened into courtship, and they quietly became engaged.

In view of the epoch's overmastering shyness in demonstrating personal affection, it is difficult to reconstruct how they ever entered into a covenant as binding as marriage. Clover hinted broadly that if the brother of a friend had not departed early from tea *à trois*, leaving Adams to stay on longer, nothing at all might have transpired between them. There may be clues to their courtship in *Esther*, Adams's roman à clef, published pseudonymously (as by Frances Snow Compton), in which the Clover character sends out echoes of faint but honorably agonized doubt: To her lover's passionate outburst, "I love you! I adore you! I will never let you go!" she replies, "You must . . . ! I am not good enough for you. You must love someone who has her heart in your work. . . . I shall ruin your life! I shall never satisfy you!"

On 3 March 1872, Adams wrote to his younger brother Brooks:

> On coming to know Clover Hooper, I found her so far away superior to any woman I had ever met, that I did not think it worth while to resist. I threw myself head over heels into the pursuit and succeeded in conducting the affair so quietly that this last week we became engaged without a single soul outside her immediate family suspecting it.

As much as one can reach to estimate the truth in Adams's heart, in this passage he certainly sounds like a man in love, as he did on other occasions. Yet he also felt free to analyze his intended in a letter to Charles Milnes Gaskell, his closest English confidant:

*Dr. Robert William Hooper*

"She talks garrulously, but on the whole pretty sensibly. She is very open to instruction. *We* shall improve her. She dresses badly. She decidely has humor and will appreciate *our* wit." He admitted that Clover was "certainly not handsome," but added, "She reads German — also Latin — also, I fear, a little Greek." (He *feared?*)

Clover was far more open in admitting her vulnerability. As she expressed it to her sister, whose marriage had given Ellen a sense of liberated fulfillment and who therefore encouraged Clover's expectations of happiness:

> This winter when the very cold weather came the sun began to warm me but I snapped my fingers at it & I tried to ignore it. By & by it got so warm that I tried to move & couldn't & then last Tuesday at about sunset the sun blinded me so that in real terror I put my hands up to my face to keep it away & when I took them away there sat Henry Adams holding them & the ice has all melted away & I am going to sit in the sun as long as it shines.

Clover was well aware of the horrors of emotional illness. Dr. Hooper, though not in regular practice, treated patients at the Worcester Asylum for the Insane and often took Clover with him on his visits. In view of the closeness between father and daughter, he must have discussed his more interesting cases with her. Her reactions were vivid. To her, becoming a burden to others or ending up in an asylum was much worse than dying; a quick end was infinitely preferable to a lingering illness. She criticized the Episcopalian practice of praying to be delivered from sudden death, as if the burden of an asylum were not worse. It is often forgotten that throughout the last century mental disorders were no less common or incurable than diphtheria, yellow fever, or tuberculosis. Rarely was even a famous family untouched: Hawthorne, Poe, Melville, the wife of Abraham Lincoln, the brothers of Emerson and Walt Whitman, all suffered the ravages of psychological collapse. The three children of Robert and Ellen Hooper would be suicides. Clover's father favored her engagement to Henry Adams, whose difficult brother Charles Francis, remarking that "all the Hoopers were crazy as coots," warned that Clover would probably kill herself. Henry remained imperturbable: "I know better than anyone the risks I run. But I have weighed them carefully and accept them," he said. The Adamses themselves were not immune to the nineteenth-century syndrome of emotional illness. Henry's brother Brooks, who confessed to his fiancée that he was "eccentric almost to the point of madness," would later have problems of his own with mental imbalance. And intermittent euphoric and schizoid fantasies were not entirely absent from Henry's mind.

In that election year of 1872, a fair possibility obtained that Henry's father would be nominated for the presidency by the Republican party. Grant's first administration was mired in scandal, though whether or not he was culpable was not known. The senior Adams had served in Congress, was a seasoned diplomat, and, as an example of the ancient probity and uncommon common sense possessed by the founding fathers, was an appealing figure. But quite in keeping with the arrogance of his clan, he refused to campaign for his party's nomination and went off to Geneva without apology. Grant was reelected by a million votes.

On 27 June, Henry Adams married Marian Hooper at her father's house in Beverly Farms, on Boston's North Shore. He had lived with Dr. Hooper for some weeks before the wedding. The ceremony, which the couple designed for and by themselves, took two minutes. Dr. Hooper lent them a nearby cottage for a fortnight's honeymoon. The bemused groom justified his insistence on seclusion to Gaskell in England: "We must be allowed to do what we think best. From having no mother to take responsibility off her shoulders, [my young woman] has grown up to look after herself and has a certain vein of personality which approaches eccentricity. This is very attractive to me but then I am absurdly in love."

One may assume that young Mr. and Mrs. Adams were reasonably happy at once and for at least a dozen years. Their childlessness has been the subject of fruitless speculation, imputed equally to physical or psychological causes. The genetic strain of mental imbalance, marked on the Sturgis side and not entirely absent from the Adams family, could have been worrisome. Their lack of children did not seem to bother either of them unduly at first. Apart from her social talents and her skill at managing what would become an elaborate household, Clover was occupied as her husband's research assistant, copyist, and strategic aide, especially gifted in gaining access to archives guarded by crusty, possessive custodians.

# VII.

Two weeks after their wedding, the Adamses sailed for London, the start of a trip that would keep them abroad for a year. Their first stop was at Wenlock Abbey in Shropshire, a renovated Gothic ruin occupied by Adams's boon companion Charles Milnes Gaskell. Both guests photographed the abbey with delight, and Clover reported to her father in Boston that Gaskell was most cordial; his home, a marvel:

> Such an ideal place as this is! The ruins of an immense abbey, ivy-covered. . . . The garden . . . is full of roses, white lilies and ferns, with close-shaven lawn. . . . The drawing-room where I am now sitting [is] long, 35 feet high, with an elaborate ceiling of oak beams, black with age, polished oak floor, jet black, with an immense Persian rug. . . . I feel as if I were a 15th-century dame and newspapers, reform, and bustle were nowhere.

On her honeymoon, she began the custom of writing weekly letters to her father. Until

his death, she abandoned it only on the rare occasion of ungovernable mental stress.

In London, the young couple hunted furniture for a future home. Clover reported to her father that drawings by Rembrandt, Van Dyck, and Hogarth were expensive; fourteen by Blake, though very curious, were a bit much at one hundred pounds. The portrait of Whistler's mother at the Royal Academy was interesting, but affected. In Paris, Clover was taken to the designer Worth by Mrs. Jack Gardner, Boston's queen of collectors, whose eccentricity exceeded all. After ordering a gown, the duplicate of one done for the Grand Duchess of Würtemberg, the Adamses departed for the Low Countries and then went to Geneva for an Adams family reunion. Clover had left her wedding dress in London; dinner for thirty seemed crowded. From Dresden, she begged Dr. Hooper to send a bright red maple leaf to remind her of New England's autumn. In Berlin, she and Henry met her cousin George Bancroft, the American Minister and noted historian. The meeting was awkward: Henry had criticized one of Bancroft's books for its peculiarities of style. She was homesick, longing desperately for her father. (It is doubtful that she had ever left him emotionally.) At the American Embassy, they dined with Theodor Mommsen, whose history of Rome she knew well. Another guest was a son of one of the brothers Grimm. Adams was impressed by German archival methods, which were very advanced. As the couple prepared for a trip up the Nile, a letter from Clover's brother, who was an astute man of business, came with news of the

50

*Henry Adams aboard the* Isis

great Boston fire of 1872, which had leveled the business district. Harvard President Eliot and his treasurer had managed to scoop up two and a half million dollars from the university strongbox in State Street; Ned reported that Henry and Clover had themselves suffered a ten-thousand-dollar loss. Clover pondered the consequences: "Is it a dead loss? We've no right to growl when we've enough to eat, but I'd rather have money run away with than burnt up, 'cos then someone enjoys it. I'm going to buy a big Japanese teapot and put everything in it—a fireproof one."

The Nile adventure promised well. Clover wrote home that Henry was utterly devoted and tender. Mosques were splendid, howling dervishes picturesque. Ralph Waldo Emerson, not quite right in the head, was also in Egypt, his Concord home having burned. A worldwide campaign for funds, swollen by generous contributions from aunt Caroline Tappan and the Bancrofts, had paid for his trip. Bancroft had taken charge of the travel arrangements for the Nile journey, but Emerson considered the adventure "A perpetual humiliation, satirizing and whipping our ignorance. . . . The sphinxes scorn dunces; the obelisks, the temple walls, defy us with their histories which we cannot spell."

The Adamses spent three long months in the *Isis*, a luxurious lateen-rigged river yacht. Besides Emerson and Bancroft, several other Bostonians were also on the Nile, soaking up the glories of the pharaohs. Nevertheless, it was hardly home. In spite of

51

Clover's apparent interest in Egyptian architectural splendors, in the peculiarities of the people, in the monstrous magnificence of Abu-Simbel, it must have become evident to her husband that she was putting on a brave show. Writing from Thebes, she said, "I must confess I hate the process of seeing things which I am hopelessly ignorant of, and am disgusted at my want of curiosity. . . . But I shall leave this [letter] open for a day or two and perhaps launch forth into glowing and poetical disquisitions on Karnak."

At Karnak, her malaise, either unacknowledged loneliness or nervous anxiety, turned into what reads like depression approaching breakdown. Naturally, it was not reported as such, but there is sufficient evidence to determine its gravity. Clover's letters to her father stopped unaccountably for two weeks. In time to come, when the problem resurfaced, the crisis on the Nile came to mind as an ominous precedent. As for Emerson, then at Thebes, he seems to have summoned courage by desperation to head for home. Clover, resuming her correspondence with her father, duly recorded his departure:

> [Mr. Emerson] was not interested in Egyptian antiquities, which for a philosopher is quite shocking. I confess that temples do begin to pall — but that is an aside — so much the worse for me! How true it is that the mind sees what it has means of seeing. I get so little, while the others about me are so intelligent and cultivated that everything appeals to them.

In Cairo, she bought a Bible and pasted in the back a photograph of Henry, head bowed, ensconced in his cabin among palm fronds arranged for a Christmas celebration. The mahogany paneling and the gilded mirror document the uneasy luxury of the *Isis*. She also initialed in the back verses that seemed appropriate to her, sketching near the chapter numerals a small tau cross, Greek, with equal arms.

Nevertheless, she was soon able to declare their winter in Egypt a great success. Her complaints would always be few. Naples, Pompeii, and Amalfi revived her spirits. In Rome, there was dear Henry James, who was in town for the season to gather background for *Roderick Hudson*, a book in progress, and who also had the painful commission for a respectful biography of William Wetmore Story. Story was a tiresome sculptor, though his studio was the center of American society. Clover, calling on him with James, was not deceived: "And oh! how he does spoil nice blocks of white marble. Nothing but Sibyls on all sides, sitting, standing, legs crossed, legs uncrossed, and all with the same expression as if they smelt something wrong. . . . Mrs. Story is very stout and tells lies." James referred to his friends as "the Clover Adams." Later, he would call Clover "a perfect Voltaire in petticoats." Because of her own intransigence and her distance from an organized church, she preferred to name herself "a Buddhist or a Mormon."

52

# VIII.

ONCE back in America, the Adamses settled into a house on Marlborough Street, on landfill recently reclaimed from Boston's Back Bay. Furniture and cartons of objects and pictures were unpacked. Dr. Hooper dwelt around the corner; there was no longer need for Clover's weekly chronicles. Adams resumed his fastidious instruction in Anglo-Saxon law to a classroom of young bachelors. Much of what Harvard had previously offered as courses was a series of simple reading programs, which students were expected to absorb more or less by rote. Adams proclaimed loud distrust of received ideas and unquestioned fact. When one youth idly asked the meaning of transubstantiation, he snapped, "Oh, go look it up." A kind of radically conservative gadfly, he grew in reputation. His methods, at least as accepted by the brighter students, heightened speculative thinking; he would later be thanked for his breezy, illuminating lectures.

In the summer of 1874, which he spent preparing a new series on American politics in the colonial period (when great-grandfather John had emerged from his Quincy farm), Henry Adams feared he was growing blind. He reduced his reading and writing to a minimum. Clover read aloud to him and answered his letters. When he recovered his eyesight, she resumed her study of Greek. Churlishly, he commented that that was now quite the thing to do — for a young woman. He himself knew no Greek, and would "have to keep her in check with medieval Latin." In some exasperation, he wrote to Gaskell:

> Our young women are haunted by the idea that they ought to read, to draw, or to labor in some way, not for any such frivolous object as making themselves agreeable to society, not for simple amusement, but to "improve" their minds. They are utterly unconscious of the pathetic impossibility of improving those poor little hard, thin, wiry, one-stringed instruments which they call their minds, and which haven't range enough to master one big emotion much less to express it in words or figures.

Adams suffered from permanent ambivalence in his ratiocinations on women. There had been strong females in his lineage, from his great-grandmother the remarkable Abigail, wife of the earlier John, to Our Lady of Chartres, whom he would claim as his personal intercessor at pilgrimage end. In 1876, he was invited to give the Lowell lectures at Harvard, a heavily endowed series of great local prestige. He chose as his subject "The Primitive Rights of Women." John Lowell, the original benefactor, had specified in his will that the auditors (who were admitted gratis to the series) be "neatly dressed and of orderly behavior." No vagrants or unwashed would drowse in the lecture-hall. His stipulation virtually restricted the audience to family and friends, but the lectures gave Adams the opportunity to put his ideas in order on a topic that would occupy his mind for years to come.

In Adams's day, it was widely believed that the women of primitive, pre-Christian tribes were mere objects to be traded or sold into slavery. But Adams propounded that the women of Teutonic forest peoples had enjoyed equal standing with the men. In the Germanic legends, he discovered the birth of representative government and there he traced the genesis of independent rights for women. In the last quarter of the nineteenth century, it was something approaching lèse majesté to suggest that there was an old and valid precedent for female equality relative to politics and property. In American Indian tribes, which Adams equated with those of ancient Germany, a bride was neither slave nor property for barter but remained what she had been before. As described by Adams, that was, for the most part "A member of her own family and clan; her children followed her line of descent, and the husband belonged to her as much as she belonged to the husband. . . . In most cases she was the head of the family; her husband usually came to live with her, not she with him, and her children belonged to her clan, not to their father's." Adams reinforced his argument with further evidence. Egyptian queens were enthroned next to their royal husbands, often their brothers; Greek wives were free women; Norse wives were equally liberated. He quoted an apt passage written by Margaret Fuller in 1845: "Women could take part in the processions, the songs, the dances, or old religions; no one fancied their delicacy was impaired by appearing in public for such a cause."

*Henry Adams*

What, then, asked Adams rhetorically, had happened to make women hoopskirted, corseted, secondary citizens without political voice or professional status? His answer: "The Church!"

> The Church felt with reason that society should be taught to obey; and of all classes of society, the women . . . were obliged to learn [obedience] most thoroughly. The Church established a new ideal of feminine character, thenceforward not the proud, self-confident, vindictive woman of German tradition received the admiration and commanded the service of law and society. . . . In reprobation of these the Church raised up, with the willing cooperation of the men, the modern type of Griselda — the meek and patient, the silent and tender sufferer, the pale reflection of the Mater Dolorosa, submissive to every torture her husband could invent.

His formidable ancestor would have defied the Church's archaic strictures. In 1777, Abigail Adams wrote to her husband:

> I long to hear that you have declared an independency — and by the way in the new Code of Laws which I suppose it will be necessary for you to make I desire you would Remember the Ladies, and be more generous and favourable to them than your ancestors. Do not put such unlimited power into the hands of the Husbands. Remember all Men would be tyrants if they could. If particular care and attention is not paid to the Ladies we are determined to foment a Rebellion, and will not hold ourselves bound by any Laws in which we have no voice, or Representation.

Whatever his great gifts as teacher and historian, Adams never became the politico or the man of force he was perhaps intended to be. He was first and foremost an aesthete. It would be years before he clarified his sentiments toward the Virgin celebrated as the Gothic Mother of God. When he did, he would find that his ideas on her were in psychological and theological imbalance and in opposition to his concept of her as a force comparable to the dynamo, in 1892 the key symbol of scientific industrial progress displayed at the Chicago World's Fair and in 1900 the exhibit that drew him again and again to the Paris Exposition. W. H. Auden defined Adams's conflicting views:

> Henry Adams thought that Venus and the Virgin of Chartres were the same persons. Actually, Venus is the Dynamo in disguise, a symbol for an impersonal natural force, and Adams' nostalgic preference for Chartres to Chicago was nothing but aestheticism; he thought the disguise was prettier than the reality, but it was the Dynamo he worshiped, not the Virgin.

# IX.

The Lowell lectures completed, Adams wrote Gaskell early in 1877: "I regard my university work as essentially done. All the influence I can exercise has been exercised. The end of it is mere railing at the idiocies of a university education."

An old family friend was now secretary of state. William Evarts (an early patron of the young Augustus Saint-Gaudens) made available to Adams a desk in the State Department and the freedom to search diplomatic archives. Adams had a congenial commission from the son of Albert Gallatin to edit the correspondence of his father, who had been minister to Great Britain under John Quincy Adams. Henry had always been drawn to Washington, which, however tiny as an urban center, was a hive of political activity. Compared with Paris, London, or Berlin, it appeared as a splendidly planned but less than half-built promise of national grandeur. However, in its concentration of power, local and international, and in the vitality of its maneuverings, it had more life than a hundred Harvards or a thousand Bostons. It was wide open, crammed with every possibility, and though he was never to play the great role he felt befitted his talents and his inheritance, he was close to every level of the game there.

In all this, Clover reveled. She and Henry rented a big house and filled it with loot from their travels. They were comfortably rich and could entertain in a ritualized reciprocity of breakfasts, teas, and dinners. The house was less than two blocks away from that White House which Henry, as a boy, had half-thought he owned and one day would inhabit.

Rutherford B. Hayes was a mediocre president. At the end of November 1877, Clover condescended to be received "very simply and graciously" by Mrs. Hayes, who permitted no hard liquor in the presidential mansion. Adams found the temperature of Washington society cool but comfortable. He and Clover attracted a large circle of friends, including the ambassadors of England, Germany, China, Turkey, and Japan. It was noted that Mrs. Adams's salons were as much to keep people out as in. The Adamses dined with General Sherman, who gave Clover what she referred to as "a little talk about (American) Indians." Carl Schurz, former general and Lincoln's minister to Spain, "played Chopin as [she] had never heard it before."

The term "snob" hardly fits Clover, since the naiveté of its regard implies a blind, prejudiced sense of innate superiority. Her snobbism was a matter of delicately adjusted nuance. She kept clear of huge official dinners, whether given by the White House or by senators or congressmen. "I have instituted 5 o'clk tea every day, thereby escaping morning visitors & it's very cosy," she wrote to her father. Her gossipy letters to him were feline: A governor of Maryland lived "mainly on opium"; she was in a pet when a congressman's consort forced on her an introduction "to a certain Miss Edes whose sole

*Henry Adams*

distinction I was told was a flirtation with Vice P. Wilson of blessed memory. I made an arctic bow and walked off." She justified such rudeness as "strong but necessary," and added, "We are not official and have a right to choose our friends and associates."

Isabel Archer, in *The Portrait of a Lady*, is another of Henry James's heroines who share some of Clover's characteristics. Of Isabel, James wrote: "Her sentiments were worthy of a radical newspaper or a Unitarian preacher. . . . Her notion of the aristocratic life was simply the union of great knowledge with great liberty; the knowledge would give one a sense of duty and the liberty a sense of enjoyment." Clover reported to her father that the novelist had written her on returning to England:

> He wished, he said, his last farewell to be said to me as I seemed to him "the incarnation of my native land"—a most equivocal compliment coming from him. Am I then vulgar, dreary and impossible to live with? That's the only obvious interpretation, however self-love might look for a gentler one.

So admired, so apparently self-confident, how could she have misinterpreted what was surely intended as a sincere tribute? What insecurities, what inner turmoil did she hide

57

behind her mask of urbanity? One senses that beneath her natural warmth, charm, and wit lay a resentment toward a society that assigned women formal courtesy while holding them firmly in bondage. She helped Adams edit the Gallatin papers, but it was hardly a full-time occupation for her. They toured historic sites of colonial and revolutionary interest; they went to Niagara Falls on the railroad president's private Pullman car. She loved long walks by the dense overgrowth near the Potomac. Mornings, she rode through Rock Creek Park with Adams on Daisy, her bay mare. Lunch, at home, was early, so Henry could leave for the State Department and the Gallatin files. He returned for tea at six. They had two male and two female servants, two dogs, two horses, and no children.

The five children of John Adams, the second president, provided him with seventeen grandchildren. The senior Charles Francis Adams's two elder sons had eleven children; his two daughters, three; his two younger sons, none. As if an explanation were somehow obligatory, Henry Adams wrote to Gaskell: "I have myself never cared enough about children to be unhappy either at having them or not having them, and if it were not that half the world will never let the other half in peace, I should never think about the subject."

Clover's mother, dead at thirty-six, had had three children and was herself one of six; Clover's father was one of nine. Clover is reported once to have exploded to her cousin Anne Lathrop, "*All* women want children." Perhaps partly consoling himself, Adams wrote Gaskell: "One consequence of having no children is that husband and wife become very dependent on each other and live very much together. This is my case."

One might deduce from letters and hearsay that Clover was a hypochondriac, but there is little to suggest that she was any more so than most women of her time. A feminist might inquire why infertility was always held to be the woman's fault. In 1879, Clover learned that one of Dr. Hooper's friends, overcome by the sensation that he merited, and was enduring, eternal damnation, had committed himself to the Somerville Asylum, near Boston. She wryly commented that such a place seemed to be "the goal of every good and conscientious Bostonian, babies and insanity the two leading topics. So and So has a baby. She becomes insane and goes to Somerville, baby grows up and promptly retires to Somerville." To Clover, it was "all nonsense."

## X.

THE political and, to only a lesser degree, literary salon maintained by the Adamses from 1879 to 1885 was a sophisticated paradigm of what had been spoken, argued, and defined during the ferment of transcendentalism and abolitionism. Far more than simply social in character, it was in the real sense educational, since its atmosphere fostered an exchange of ideas and information among the best minds then serving the national destiny. Both Adamses demonstrated the Emersonian principle of "unconscious radiation of virtue" on old friends and new acquaintances alike. Their effort was more conscious than not, for both saw themselves not just in a social and political service but also as the center of a didactic reformation of taste. With the ready examples of the pictures and objects they owned they could demonstrate the excellence of past craft from Europe (since they noticed little enough of native American) and from the Orient as well, for they collected Chinese bronzes and porcelain and Japanese kakemonos and woodblock prints.

After completing his task of editing the Gallatin correspondence, Adams began to plan a monumental *History of the United States of America during the Administrations of Jefferson and Madison*, which would fill nine volumes. Research for that gigantic task, which he designed in not unjustified terms of Gibbon and Mommsen, sent him to closed archives in England and France, opened to him (though with some difficulty) through his diplomatic connections, and in Spain, to which Clover's charm and fluency in Spanish gained him access. To John Hay, who with George Nicolay had served as private secretary to Abraham Lincoln and who was then preparing with Nicolay a ten-volume biography of the Liberator, Adams wrote: "I make it a rule to strike out ruthlessly in my writings whatever my wife criticises on the theory that she is the average reader, and that her decisions are in fact if not in reason absolute."

Hay, whom Adams had met briefly in 1861, when Hay had come to Washington with Lincoln from Springfield, Illinois, had returned to the capital in 1879 as assistant secretary of state in the Hayes administration. It was then that he and Adams developed a friendship that would only be strengthened by passing years and private adversity until Hay died in 1905. Adams wrote of him to Sir Robert Cunliffe:

> I never knew more than two or three men from west of the Alleghenies who knew the difference between a gentleman and a swindler. This curious obliquity makes [Hay] a particularly charming companion to me, as he knows intimately scores of men whom I would not touch with a pole, but who are more amusing than my own crowd.

When many persons suggested that Adams's political novel *Democracy* — more of a transposed memoir than a work of fiction and published anonymously — was by *Mrs*. Henry Adams, Adams objected testily to Hay, "My wife never wrote for publication in her life and could not write if she tried." His irritation was not the expression of a total lack of generosity but rather of his belief that after long observation and analysis he knew woman's capacity, and it did not include much exercise of the mind. He liked women. He was almost obsessed with them on an ideal level, but on closer acquaintance

*John Hay*

they usually turned out to be a divinity newly married or a charming girl. As far as a clever woman (Clover) went, he wrote to Gaskell: "Her mind only fed on itself and was neither happy nor altogether free from morbid self-reflections which always come from isolation in society, as I know to my cost."

In the face of that self-satisfied complacency, with her husband enjoying his compulsive labors, how should a wife occupy herself? Clover took up Portuguese. Her sister was then helping to turn the Harvard Annex into Radcliffe College, and Clover sent cash and moral support. She was instrumental in founding in Charleston, South Carolina, cradle of the Confederacy, an art school "to help educate and cultivate a vanquished foe." And there were letters to father, constant entertaining, supervising a household, and acquiring pictures, mostly watercolors and drawings by Mantegna, Rembrandt, Rubens, Blake, and Bonington. She dared to purchase two small portraits by Sir Joshua Reynolds, although Adams loathed all "face-painting." Clover's response: "Henry can look the other way."

A considerable infusion of warmth came from a little club called the Five of Hearts, which met at the Adamses' house. Clover had her notepaper engraved at the top with a tiny playing card. The club's sole members were the two Adamses, the two Hays, and Clarence King. King, a geologist and a promoter of mining development, was a fascinating man and a true eccentric who, Hay said, had profound sympathy for "the most wretched derelicts of civilization," American Indians and southern blacks in particular; he had a clandestine, common-law marriage with a black woman. Except for Hay and

60

Gaskell, he was Adams's closest friend. He was extremely fond of Clover and understood her apparent strangeness.

In 1881, Clover's sister-in-law Fanny, having given birth to five daughters in seven years, became seriously ill and died. Clover had wished to nurse her. Because the family wanted to spare Clover upset, they managed to keep her from the funeral by informing her of Fanny's death by slow mail instead of by telegram. At around the same time, Adeline Bigelow, a cousin with whom Clover had made two trips to Europe, suffered a bad nervous breakdown, a peril she herself had guessed at. Clover wrote, "I cannot bear to think that what she most feared has come to pass—for such sweet cheery creatures it seems a cruel fate. . . . I wish it might have been Worcester [the asylum with which Dr. Hooper was connected] instead of Somerville which is such a smelly hideous place."

By 1882, Adams, surrounded by hints and threats of mortality, was recording an endemic decline among his peers:

> Hay had heart palpitations; King suffered from an old rupture; Richardson had "Bright's disease" [and would soon die]; Wendell Holmes was "very weary" [and would live for decades]; Louis Agassiz, "another invalid"; not to mention the state of my brother Brooks [who was suffering from writer's block]. . . . These are the jewels of my generation, all the friends I have that count in life.

Amasa Stone, Clara Hay's father, a prosperous railroad builder, made a decision in constructing a bridge that resulted in its collapse, carrying a trainload of people to their deaths. Under the strain of the charges against him, his health was destroyed and in 1883 he ended his own life.

The ethics of suicide, with its questionable license, had long been a subject of discussion among prickly, hyperconscious New Englanders who from Cotton Mather, through Emerson, to the senior Henry James steadfastly verbalized their intellectual, personal, epistemological, theological beliefs in the permanent dissatisfaction that was their torment and triumph.

Around 1867, Alice James, maiden daughter of Henry the philosopher and sister of Henry the novelist, had begun to show manic-depressive and hysterical symptoms that could grow into certifiable insanity. She was victimized by fantasies—herself "knocking off the head of the benignant Pater, as he sat with his silver locks, writing." Self-slaughter was also in mind as an increasingly magnetic option. Was suicide a sin? Was it right? Was it wrong? Pray, papa, tell me. After due consideration, he judged it was indeed permissible for her to choose to end her existence, if it was with a view to break bonds or to assert her freedom and as long as she could arrange it in a perfectly gentle way in order not to distress her friends. Nevertheless, though Alice could perceive it to be her right to dispose of her own body when life had become intolerable, she could never do it. Instead, for the rest of her years she took refuge in a series of imaginary illnesses.

In Adams's book *Democracy*, the character Madeleine Lee, based on Clover, is self-doomed and patently suicidal. To avoid any proximity to facts too close to the bone, Adams portrayed her as losing her husband and, within a week, her only child. A friend of Madeleine's describes her reaction: "She was wild with despair . . . almost insane. Indeed I have always thought she was quite insane for a time. I knew she was excessively violent and wanted to kill herself, and I never heard anyone rave as she did about religion and resignation and God."

Mental illness hovered like an ominous mist. On 2 July 1881, President James A. Garfield was shot in the back by Charles Julius Guiteau, a member of the Oneida Community, a religious society established in central New York in 1848 by John Humphrey Noyes. The assassin had felt inspired by the Deity to remove Garfield. His defense would be palpable insanity, substantiated by a long prior list of litigations, protests, and general depravity. A few liberal neurologists, not yet able to arm their defense by psychiatric precedents, pointed to Guiteau's deformed skull and genetic history. Adams was much involved with the nature of heredity; a part of the continuing process of his "education":

> To an American in search of a father, it mattered nothing whether the father breathed through lungs, or walked on fins, or on feet. Evolution of mind was altogether another matter and belonged to another science, but whether one traced descent from the shark or the wolf was immaterial even in morals. This matter had been discussed for ages without scientific result. La Fontaine and other fabulists maintained that the wolf, even in morals, stood higher than man; and in view of the late civil war, Adams had doubts of his own on the facts of moral evolution.

Guiteau needed an eye examination and the oculist, a Dr. Folsom, invited Adams and Clover to accompany him to the prison. Clover did not recognize the man who, mistaking Adams for the doctor, rose from his chair. Thinking he was a jailor, she shook the murderer's hand. She wrote her father, "I don't wish to have it repeated that I shook hands with the accursed beast, without the context being given. Someone would write that they 'were sorry to hear that I had asked Guiteau to tea.'"

Henry Adams had his own insights on insanity. After observing Guiteau's trial for some days, he wrote to Wayne MacVeagh, who, in his post as attorney general in Garfield's cabinet, had secured the indictment of the president's assassin:

> Why is the District Attorney so eager to prove Guiteau sane? You can't hang him. Your only chance for shutting him up for life is to prove him *not* sane. More than this, the

assertion that Guiteau is sane is a gross insult to the whole American people. . . . The peculiarity of insanity is the lack of relation between cause and effect. . . . That he is rational proves nothing. We are all more or less rational; it is an almost invariable sign of insanity.

Guiteau went to the gallows swearing it had been God's act, not his. During his trial, in which he insisted on defending himself, he behaved as wildly as possible. That struck many as a determined effort to prove his madness, inherited or not. Clover, who had attended the trial, reported to Dr. Hooper: "The assassin was in front of me, so I could only get his profile — a large strong nose, a high straight forehead. . . . He bullied and badgered everyone; banged his fist on the table. . . . The beast's sallies are more than unjudicial muscles can stand. . . . Every word that Guiteau says tightens his noose now."

Adams's analytical intelligence might have admitted the possibility of a genetic lapse, but Clover was a good Emersonian. If there was no free will, no choice among the multitude of options, where did that leave her? Indeed, where did that leave anyone? On the last day of Guiteau's trial, she wrote her father, "The witnesses that day smashed the hereditary insanity theory pretty thoroughly." Nevertheless, it is interesting to note that Guiteau's mother had died of "brain fever" when Guiteau was seven, and that his whole youth was marked by obstreperous nervousness. Noyes, the head of the Oneida Community, considered him insane, as did his own father.

# XI.

BOTH Clover and Adams indulged in photography from early days. On their Nile journey, they carried an elaborate, unwieldy mechanism; each took pictures of the sights and of one another. In those days, technical procedures were so experimental that to distinguish between the professionals and those who used cameras for fun was difficult. The photographic process required a fiendishly painstaking attention and called for as much mechanical and chemical expertness as visual. A freshly washed glass plate brushed evenly with collodion and with a mixture of guncotton dissolved in ether and alcohol produced a gluelike surface, which, when soaked in silver nitrate, received the image from the lens. The wet glass was slid into a sealed shield and inserted into the camera. The subject, properly set, posed, and warned, could not budge for a count of light-determined seconds. Then, the plate went back to the darkroom to be developed: dipped first in a bath of acid; next in a fixing agent — Clover used potassium cyanide — then in clear running water. As often as not, the final image could be blanked or blurred by the capricious sun.

Photography had developed into a universally popular service. Congress began to support Mathew Brady's Gallery of Illustrious Americans by 1850. For forty years, before the Civil War and after, Brady's labors and those of his colleagues contributed unforgettable visual reminders of their era. Clover joined a photographic society and trained herself to be more than a capable amateur. In 1883, she sent her father a review of an exhibition in which portraits she had shown were classed as "very skillful." By that December, she was so busy developing recent work that her weekly chronicle to her father was late:

> It was science plain & simple which took up all my morning on Sunday & left me sleepy in the p.m. A wonderful process of printing from negatives has been perfected lately & the man who owns the patent gave an exhibition of the process at the photographic rooms in the National Museum on Sunday. Mr. C. Richardson very kindly smuggled me in as the only woman — we were three hours there though the process is really very rapid. I shall buy of Siebert the right to use his patent for a trifle and will send you a proof.

Perhaps at last Clover had found a device for competing with her husband on his own terms: as a historian, taking pictures of the principal personages of her time, providing an exact and living record. She was close to a broad range of illustrious friends and relatives. From her capturings of the architect Henry Hobson Richardson, the painter John La Farge, Oliver Wendell Holmes as a young jurist, the historians Francis Parkman and George Bancroft, we derive a fresh, sensitive approximation of their appearance as their contemporaries saw them. Accompanied by her husband, she took her paraphernalia to C Street to photograph Senator Lucius Q. C. Lamar:

> Printed photos for nearly two hours — seizing a bright sun which is rare of late — then H & I drove to Senator Lamar's rooms . . . to take his photo. L. brushed his long hair to the regulation smoothness & then I refused to take his likeness until he had rumpled it all up. I took two shots of him & one of Gordon [a general from Georgia] who has a deep hole from Antietam in his left cheek as you'll see next summer.

The war was a living memory. She photographed the endless ranks of small, identical marble headstones in the Arlington National Cemetery: "We rode to Arlington Friday P.M. and it was lovely with its fifteen thousand quiet sleepers; no unsightly iron flummery and granite lies there, there's no lovelier place in the world as I know it than Arlington with a sunset behind it and a view in front."

In Clover's last seven months of existence, there was an almost feverish urgency in taking and developing the glass plates. She kept careful notes, not just of subjects but of lengths of exposure, weather conditions, and reasons for success or failure: "Francis Parkman in front of Rocks at Beverly Farms, large stop, 2 seconds. . . . Jan. 18, 1884.

*Henry Adams and Marquis*

H. H. Richardson in Henry Adams' study, large stop, 10 seconds — good." Henry Adams was caught in sharp profile, seated on steps, holding Marquis, a big Skye terrier who, along with Possum and Boojum, was a family retainer. Unrelaxed, one hand under the dog's chin, Adams offers nothing of a full face; his mute stare declares ungraciousness. And there is Dr. Hooper, neat in his derby hat, seated on his buckboard drawn by Kitty the mare. Turned three-quarters toward Clover's camera, as she probably placed him, he is casually comfortable.

Among her portraits, particularly evocative are those of George and Elizabeth Bancroft. Clover admitted that while she considered them technically acceptable, they were, perhaps, "not pleasant likenesses." Her historian cousin, seated, quill in hand, annotates from an open volume. There are two of Mrs. Bancroft, a formidable old lady and a Sturgis connection. In one, she is in half-shadowed full face; in the other, she is seen in urgent profile (her photographer was reminded of a marble bust of Judge Davis in the gallery of the Boston Athenaeum). The print of Bancroft impressed John Hay so much that he urged Richard Watson Gilder, editor of *The Century*, a magazine of wide circulation, to use it and to ask Adams to write a short accompanying article. Reproduction might have led to other commissions and something approaching a professional career. Adams forbade it. As he put it in a letter to Hay: "We have declined Mr. Gilder's pleasing offer. You know our modesty. . . . As for flaunting our photographs in *The Century*, we should expect to experience the curses of all our unphotographed friends."

In the lonely months to come, Adams may have had occasion to feel a twinge of remorse over his automatic denial of her opportunity. His excuse was nonsense. Bancroft was forty years older than he and a well-known historian. Clover reported the incident to Dr. Hooper without a trace of chagrin:

> Yesterday I was amused to get a letter from R.W. Gilder, the editor of *The Century* magazine, asking if I would let him have a photo of Mr. Bancroft. Someone had spoken to him of it with a view to its reproduction in the magazine & writing Henry to write an article on Papa Bancroft of 7 or 8 pages to go with it. I've just written to decline & telling him Mr. Adams does not fancy the prevailing literary vivisection. The way in which Howells butters Henry James, & Henry James, Daudet, & Daudet someone else is not pleasant. The mutual admiration game is about played out or ought to be.

Adams had toyed with photography, but had small use for the medium as anything approaching an art form. When Ralph Waldo Emerson confessed that camera work gave him more pleasure than hand-painted pictures, Adams reproved him for demonstrating either "extreme sublimation or tenuity of intelligence." After Clover's death, he avowed: "I hate photographs abstractly because they have given me more ideas perversely and immovably wrong, than I should ever get by imagination."

If indeed Adams harbored some skulking envy of his wife's brave efforts toward a measure of independence, it would hardly have been the sole factor in his putative guilt. After she died, he burned every single letter Dr. Hooper had written her over the years. How could Adams ignore the indissoluble link with her father? In *Esther*, the novel he published pseudonymously a year before their deaths, his fictional characters behaved as their prototypes may well have done in reality. The father-in-law wishes the young husband dead. When he does die, Esther, in despair, wants "to escape, to turn away, to get out of life itself rather than suffer such pain, such terror, such misery of helplessness."

Whatever bearing Clover's reading of Schopenhauer may have had on her, the author, a man whose father had killed himself, could at least determine despair in a manner she could comprehend:

> Hope is the confusion of the desire for a thing with its probability. . . . He who is without hope is also without fear: this is the meaning of the expression "desperate." For it is natural to man to believe true what he desires to be true, and to believe it because he desires it; if this salutary and soothing quality in his nature is obliterated by repeated ill-fortune, and he is even brought to the point of believing that what he does not desire must happen and what he desires to happen can never happen simply because he desires it, then this is the condition called despair.

*George Bancroft*

*Elizabeth Davis Bancroft*

# XII.

AROUND Christmastime 1883, the Adamses decided to build a house of their own, a permanent, luxurious establishment to replace their usual rentals. There was a large, empty lot on the corner of 11th and 16th streets, directly facing the White House across Lafayette Park. John Hay, who had come into money, was happy to join them in plans for a large double mansion to be designed by Richardson, great architect and reviver of the Romanesque, who had known Adams since college. Trinity Church in Boston, its portal echoing that of Saint-Trophîme in Arles, was Richardson's masterpiece. During its construction, young Augustus Saint-Gaudens assisted in the mural decorations, painting the figures of the saints Paul and James, and Sir Edward Burne-Jones and John La Farge designed stained-glass windows. On a visit to New York earlier in 1883, Clover visited Saint-Gaudens's studio. He happened to be absent, but she saw work-in-progress on the memorial to her cousin Robert Gould Shaw. That was fourteen years before the great bronze relief was unveiled and during a period of labor so prolonged that the sculptor all but lost the commission. She was delighted that the contract had not gone to William Wetmore Story, as Senator Charles Sumner had first proposed.

The joined houses resembled something of a domestic fortress, vaguely Romanesque in the architect's revived, transformed manner. Richardson had already built a stone summer house at Prides Crossing for Clover's sister. Although extremely busy with important buildings under construction, notably the monumental Allegheny County Courthouse in Pittsburgh, and with his design for All Saints Cathedral in Albany, he eventually arrived in Washington and cast a cool eye on Adams's own inch-to-the-foot scale drawings of what he thought he wanted. Richardson suffered from nephritis, which would soon carry him off. Clover's photograph of the architect suggests Adams's description of him as a "man-mountain [Gargantua]." (On another occasion, he called him "an ogre [who] devours men crude, and shows the effect of inevitable indigestion in his size.") Richardson's extravagant use of fine materials was no secret. The luxury he loved lent itself to detailed, elaborate stone, executed with careful craftsmanship. Clover was concerned about costs:

> We think that as we know just what we want and don't want in the new house that Richardson will consider our wishes. Our present furniture and fittings pitch the key note beforehand. We cannot have a mahogany dining room with our present black walnut and cherry furniture nor can we go in for carving without making what we have seem *mesquin*.

*Mesquin*? There would be nothing shabby or niggardly about the palatial joint residence, with its ground floor seemingly designed more for show than for living. The

68

last months of Clover's life held an acceleration of omens. A large section of the parlor ceiling of the Adamses' rented house fell one morning, just before breakfast. She wrote, "If we had been early risers we should have been corpses inevitably." That event added impetus to their prolonged impatience at the architect's constant procrastination.

Their own house, compared with Hay's adjoining, was relatively simple, according to Adams's taste, and lacked the turrets and gables of what Clover termed Richardson's "agnostic" style. After rejecting any use of hand-cut stone, changing basic materials from sandstone to brick, she allowed for a bit of sculptured detail, "as the devout do in their churches." It must have been something of a foregone conclusion that when the house was finished Adams would complain that he felt Hay's home to be the more successful of the two. He was answered with the professional's eternal justification: "Your liking Hay's house better than your own is accounted for easily I think by the fact that in designing the former I was left entirely untrammelled by restrictions wise or other-

*Henry Hobson Richardson*

wise." While the Adamses waited for final plans and for contracts to be signed, their own establishment had to be run; with constant arrival and departure of guests, it resembled a family hotel. In what time was left, there was always Clover's photography.

In the windy sleet and rain of March 1885, news came that Clover's father was stricken with angina, a condition then ominous in a man of seventy-four. Adams, in *Esther*, which in so many details cannot help but seem prophetic, describes his heroine's apprehension:

> She knew that there was no hope and that her father himself was only anxious for the end, yet to see him suffer and slowly fade out was terrible. . . . Esther had been told she must not give way to agitation, under the risk of killing her father, who lay dozing, half-conscious, with his face turned towards her. Whenever his eyes opened they rested on hers.

Clover left for Cambridge at once, and for the next month shared sickroom service with her sister's and brother-in-law's family. In thirteen years of marriage, she and Henry had never been separated. Though he wrote nearly every day, his letters were awkwardly apologetic in tone. He commenced painfully, or pitifully, with an inverted courtesy that might have caused her dismay if she had been less preoccupied:

> Madam: As it is now thirteen years since my last letter to you, you may have forgotten my name. If so try to recall it. For a time we were somewhat intimate. . . . There remains at the bottom of the page just a little crumb of love for you, but you must not eat it all at once. The dogs need some.

Certainly, it was meant well. In his way, he loved her. As her absence extended, his artificial chill warmed. He was busying himself over finishing the new house. He had searched the Smithsonian's mineral collection for the perfect porphyry for facing the living-room fireplace. As for her own bathroom: if a good wall-yellow was not available, how about red? An elevator, a safe, and a burglar alarm were installed. Stairs were in work. Only after Clover's urging did he finally consent to attend one of President Cleveland's dinners, taking Richardson along with him. Rose Cleveland, the president's daughter, received them. As Adams related in a letter to Clover, she then:

> . . . took us into the red room where we found the president seated in a melancholy way. . . . We must admit that, like Abraham Lincoln, the Lord made a mighty common-looking man in him. . . . Miss Cleveland carries an atmosphere of female college about her, thicker than the snow storm outside my window. She listens seriously and asks serious questions. . . . I have seldom been more amused than in thus meeting a sister professor in "the first lady of the land." I liked her. . . . I explained why you were not with me, and she cordially asked me to bring you over in the evening.

70

Dutifully, Adams visited Cambridge, staying as few hours as possible, returning to devoted dogs. He finally managed to admit that Clover was missed, and by him as well. How, he asked, had he "ever managed to hit on the only woman in the world who fits my cravings and never sounds hollow anywhere?" He added, with customary austerity, that he did not expect to have to wait long alone. Nor did he. Dr. Hooper died three days later, on 13 April. Clover wrote John Hay's wife: "His humor and courage lasted till unconsciousness came and he went to sleep like a tired traveler."

On her father's desk, Clover found a fragment that he'd kept, perhaps salvaged from the memoirs of an aristocrat of l'ancien régime, one who had survived the Terror: "In that time, one knew how to live and die; one didn't have the excuse of inconvenient illnesses. If one caught gout, one nevertheless walked on without making a face; one concealed suffering under a good education."

After her deathwatch and return to Washington, Adams noticed that she seemed tired, but, contrary to what might have been feared, her spirits appeared to be improving. She wisely resolved not to spend the summer at Beverly Farms. For her, New England was now a dead land. Inquiries were made about the recently opened Yellowstone National Park and about the possibility of spending six weeks camping out in the Rockies. However, early summer was blackfly season, so, with their two horses, Adams and Clover drove to the huge old resort hotel at Sweet Springs, West Virginia. Though it was capable of hosting nearly a thousand guests, they found it on opening day all but empty. Adams wrote to Gaskell:

> A country less known to Bostonians could not be found. . . . On our first ride we nearly fell off our horses at seeing hillsides sprinkled with flaming yellow, orange and red azaelias, all mixed together, and masses of white and pink laurel. . . . On our second ride, we got a long way into the mountains by a rough path, and the groves of huge rhododendrons were so gloomy and shook their dark fingers so threateningly over our heads, that we turned about and fled for fear night should catch us, and we should never be seen any more by our dear enemies.

By July, the blackflies were gone, and they planned to entrain for Yellowstone with luxurious baggage and equipment, twelve pack animals, and a cook. But, Adams now confided to Gaskell, "We [*sic*] broke down"; his wife had been out of sorts, and "until she gets quite well again, [we] can do nothing." So, ill-advisedly, they went to Beverly Farms.

On their return to Washington, Clover, in the absence of any effective therapy, was locked in a wall of ice, condemned to loneliness and lassitude. She tried to endure her obsessive fantasies of guilt — of what she had done, of what she had failed to do. But she felt she was more Stoic than Christian and must support her failings without a word. She clung to her sister, who recalled: "She was so tender and humble — and appealing when no human help could do anything — sorry for every reckless word or act, wholly forgotten by all save her. Her constant cry was 'Ellen I'm not real — oh make me real — You all of you — are real!'"

There was a disturbing incident concerning Richardson's placement of a block of freshly carved sandstone plumb between the two arches that formed the entrance to the new houses. The carving was of an Assyrian lion backed by a tau cross, perhaps recalling the ensign of the Venetian Republic's extremissima serenity. Adams was furious; he wanted the workmen to cease and desist. Hay was not troubled; he felt the carving to be magnificently successful. Adams replied that he began to "turn red, blue and green of nights thinking about it and hiding my head under my pillow. . . . I wish the Assyrian animal would walk off and carry the cross back to the British Museum." He begged Richardson to have the monster removed. He was flatly refused. He sulked in silence, consoling himself that the decoration was in the worst of all possible taste, *really*! That it could have been proposed as a lucky sign of faith by someone near and dear to him never suggested itself. Why the architect felt free to go against his client's express command, why Hay claimed wholehearted approval, remains a mystery. Recently, it has been suggested that the traditional symbol of Saint Mark was a private gesture of Clover's confided to two of her most understanding friends.

Clover spent waking hours and sleepless nights in her prison of apology and guilt. In her tenuous faith there was little consolation. A neighbor knocked daily to offer the placebo of gossip, trying to pull a distraught, mourning woman out of the depths. Charles Francis Adams recalled that his last encounter with his sister-in-law had been painful to a degree. He had never cared for her. His early warnings concerning her sanity had been ignored. At the start of December, she appeared to improve; a few friends thought there was a good change. On 6 December, a Sunday, the day she had once written her weekly reports to her father, Clover and Henry breakfasted together. He had toothache and went for a dentist. At the door, he encountered a woman caller and he returned to see if Clover wished to receive her. She did not, and he went out. Clover started a letter to her sister: "If I had one single point of character or goodness I would stand on that and grow back to life. Henry is more patient and loving than words can express. God might envy him — he bears and hopes and despairs hour after hour. . . . Henry is beyond all words tenderer and better than all of you even."

The letter stayed unfinished. Clover went into her darkroom and took the bottle of potassium cyanide. Less than an hour later, Henry found her, still warm, in front of her fireplace. He carried her to a chaise longue and ran for a doctor. Her body was contorted, and the room had the cloying odor of bitter almonds.

# XIII.

CLOVER was buried in earth over which she and Adams had so often cantered. He disdained all habiliments of grief. On the Monday after her death, sister Ellen and Ephraim, her husband, dined with Adams. He was sporting a red cravat, and he ripped the black mourning band off his sleeve and tossed it under the table.

In the following days, he reduced action to the minimum; he shifted books from shelf to table; he read Hamlet and Lear. When John Hay, then in New York, wired his eager willingness to come to Washington to help, Adams replied:

> Nothing you can do will affect the fact that I am left alone in the world at a time of life when too young to die and too old to take up existence afresh; but after the first feeling of desperation is over, there will be much that you can do to make my struggle easier. I am going to keep straight on. . . . Never fear for me, I shall come all right from this — what shall I call it — Hell!

Hay's attempt at condolence was no more than that of many who, in profoundest sincerity on such a dreaded, helpless, and hopeless occasion, uttered what they could. He and his wife had also loved her:

> Is it any consolation to remember her as she was? That bright intrepid spirit, that keen fine intellect, that lofty scorn of all that was mean, that social charm which made your house such a one as Washington never knew before, and made hundreds of people love her, as much as they admired her. No, that makes it all the harder to bear.

Adams soon moved into the fortress Richardson had raised for the two of them; for the rest of a long life he would live and work in it alone. In one sense, however dismaying, he was free. He and Clover had met Elizabeth Cameron, the very young, beautiful wife of the much older Senator James Donald (Don) Cameron, who for the next forty years would be Clover's passionate replacement. There were those who tried to attach ignoble significance to her relationship with Adams even before Clover's death, yet there is no shred of evidence to sustain it. The last call Clover made outside her house was on Mrs. Cameron, who was sick abed. And it would be some five years, only after his first disconsolate wanderings, before Mrs. Cameron began to provide him with the most emotionally satisfying friendship he was ever to know.

He sent to the printers the first half of his great study of the nation's two early administrations. Friends were relieved to remark the recovery of his customary tone. His efforts to maintain a steady course, pursuing life as he could and must, were stoic and characteristic. In proof of his resolve, he decided on a trip to Japan, exactly as he and Clover had once proposed.

A logical move. First, there was the healthy ocean voyage; then, Clover's cousin William Sturgis Bigelow was teaching English in Tokyo. (Finding complete peace in oriental custom, he later converted to Buddhism.) Japanese art had long provided objects for Adams's home, and Ambassador Baron Yoshida had become a friend. But there were hindrances, too. Richardson kept fussing over the completion of the twin houses, all but finished, yet unfurnished. Important details were still to be considered. As long before as 1 October 1885, Adams had complained to Hay: "No Mikado for me yet. If I run away and hide in Japan, can I furnish from there?" He hated to travel alone. Clarence King was in England, hunting cash for his mining investments. Young Alex Agassiz, Louis's son and a charming youth, had just returned from India and would not soon again leave home.

However, there was Adams's old friend John La Farge. The painter had reached a stalemate in a big mural he was designing for Manhattan's Tenth Street Church of the Ascension, frustrated by his attempts to paint angels that would appear to be hovering in the air and by the absence of an appropriate landscape background. Perhaps the mountainous scenery of Kyushu and Shikoku might offer data. La Farge was not rich. Adams was delighted to pay. The painter was a devout Roman Catholic, his manner and habits quite amazingly abstemious. Adams was content that this much-desired companion "unlike most men of genius . . . had no vices I could detect." Gifted as both a painter and innovative master in stained glass, La Farge was a fortuitous complement to Adams. They had in common a New England upbringing and a tolerance for separate temperamental quirks. La Farge endured bad nerves, sleeplessness, and dyspepsia, which his wife named "diplomatic illnesses." He confessed, "[My] temper is frightful and the world is stuffed with sawdust." Adams was familiar with such sentiments. La Farge told him he reasoned too much. Hence, the Japanese adventure was anticipated as a virtual rest cure: the two agreed to bring no books, read no books, but go as innocently as they could. That was entirely disingenuous. Adams was better acquainted than most with Japanese thought and art, even better than those men whose fortunes had been in part made from trade with the Orient. La Farge was a pioneer amateur author of a study of Japanese painting, an art he praised highly for the marvelous decoration and intellectual refinement of its color. He was forced to grant, however, that the subtlest, deepest, and most complicated feelings of the mind, which were inherent in Christian art, were as lacking in the Orient as in classical Greece or imperial Rome.

Adams and Clover had sought dealers in paintings, porcelains, and prints in London and Paris. In Washington, Baron Yoshida had invited them to a demonstration of the tea ceremony and the Chinese Ambassador Chen-Lau Pi had told Adams of his nation's ancient legal institutions. Adams's personal interest in the Orient dated to before his marriage. Restless and bored with family fame and its indicated potential, he had

*Unknown photographer. John La Farge, ca. 1895*

dreamed of islands beyond the broad Pacific. The Meiji revolt of 1867 opened Japan to its emergence as a modern industrial power having imperial ambitions. Now there would be an infusion of bustles, sewing machines, pianos, railroads, and men-of-war. Adams, as a philosophizing historian, must have been fascinated by the spectacle of drastic change from feudal tyranny to a constitutional monarchy. What could be more paradoxical than a land supposedly disciplined by the tenets of Northern Buddhism's self-annihilation now overtaken by frantic industrialization and a hasty assimilation of scientific materialism? But it was not politics but art that drew Adams to the East.

Before he left the United States, a secret remained to be disclosed. To John Hay and Clarence King, twin dearest of Clover's Five of Hearts, he confessed to having written *Democracy* and *Esther*. The mystery of their authorship must have weighed heavily on him, especially in view of their prophetic anticipations of tragedy, their events and characters paralleling the reality of his life and Clover's.

On 11 June 1886, Adams wrote John Hay from San Francisco:

Our journey was a glorious success. As I got into my train at Boston on Thursday the 3rd, my brother Charles [president of the Union Pacific Railroad] came down to tell me that his directors' car would return [empty] to Omaha the next day. So I went to New York rejoicing; passed a delightful day with King, St Gaudens &c, and at 6 P.M. dragged poor La Farge, in a dishevelled and desperate, but still determined mind, on board the Albany express.

It was perhaps at that farewell meeting that the proposal to make some memorial to Clover was first broached. It would be only after Adams and La Farge had returned from Japan, however, that notions were sufficiently formed to give the sculptor some hint of what was even then only vaguely defined. During the cross-country journey, Adams immersed himself in Buddhist texts of meditations on the terrestrial and celestial existence of Gautama-Buddha and on precepts of the Four Noble Truths and the Noble Eightfold Path.

At Omaha, Nebraska, the train, empty of passengers save for Adams and La Farge, stopped. A reporter from a local newspaper, attracted by the splendor of the solitary directors' car, sought an interview. As Adams wrote Hay, "When in reply to his inquiry as to our purpose in visiting Japan, La Farge beamed through his spectacles the answer that we were in search of Nirvana, the youth looked up like a meteor and rejoined: 'It's out of season.'"

Nirvana, Nibana, Nibwanna, however writ in Adams's subsequent mentions, is the key to the rest of this account. What Adams thought he meant when he referred to Nirvana, and to Brahma, Buddha, and Kwannon, is as difficult to determine as it is to condense into a short passage objective, philosophical, and historically comprehensive definitions of those terms. Nevertheless, a brief discussion of them may be useful here.

## XIV.

THE Hindu Upanishads, "The Reality of the Real," formulated around the sixth century B.C., the same moment as the advent of Pythagoras, Confucius, and Zoroaster, are the first recorded attempts at a systematic organization of thought in India. Their influence ultimately spread Buddhism throughout Asia.

The essence of the Upanishads lies in the relationship or equivalency of the *atman* — the individual, particularized self — to *brahman*, the primordial, absolute One. The true Brahmin, that is, the true follower of Brahmanism, recognizes this unity and must come to the understanding that every self is part of that One and bears the Absolute invisibly within him. Understanding leads to a fusion of *atman* and *brahman*, overcoming the division between an individual and his eternal source. *Brahman* is neuter, neither god nor goddess; without attributes, form, or task; omnipresent yet imperceptible. It is the transcendent being that penetrates, vivifies, and supports the universe. In this respect, *brahman* corresponds to the Buddhist *Nirvana*, about which one can affirm nothing.

> Monks, there is a domain where there is neither solid nor fluid, neither heat nor movement, neither this world nor that, neither sun nor moon. Monks, I call that neither a coming nor a going, nor a stopping, nor a being born nor a dying. It is without any foundation, without development, without foothold. That is what the end of suffering is.*

At the commencement of the nineteenth century, Arthur Schopenhauer, among others, promulgated a pessimistic interpretation of practical Buddhism, derived from initial translations from the original Sanskrit, which emphasized but a single aspect of how Nirvana might be attained. This he construed as "denial of the will."

*The Light of Asia: The Teacher of Nirvana and the Law*, a prolix Indian epic by Sir Edwin Arnold, appeared in 1879 and was continually reprinted. Of its 1883 edition, Lafcadio Hearn, an influential Japanologist, wrote: "After all, Buddhism in some esoteric form may prove the religion of the future. . . . What are the heavens of all Christian fancies after all but Nirvana — the extinction of individuality in the eternal."

Arnold's poem, which dealt with Buddha's career, was disdained by experts as partial, false, or both. Victorian theologians were shocked by an implicit identification of a "heathen" Gautama Buddha with the Second Person of the Trinity. All parallels between Buddhism and Gospel Christianity, either from the viewpoint of Roman Catholicism, Protestant Episcopalianism, or Unitarian transcendentalism are essentially confusing unless cautiously defined. Buddhism and its mutation from Brahmanism are practical proposals more ethical and psychological than philosophical or theological. There was never reason for the followers of Buddhism to work out a complete or quasiscientific theory of "personality"; the problem was to set moral continuity as the basis for human development. Buddhism makes no real claim to mystical revelation; its metaphors are poetic but hardly metaphysical.

Henry Adams certainly educated himself in these matters beyond texts and their commentaries through his conversations with Baron Yoshida, Ernest Fenollosa, Sturgis Bigelow, the Japanese art historian Okakura Kakuzo, and La Farge. His personal use of words signifying Brahman or Buddhist ideas became more defined only later, when La Farge, far better informed than he on oriental thought and art, transmitted comprehensible concepts to Saint-Gaudens at work in his studio on the memorial. Whatever his attraction to the exotic or the aesthetic, Adams was no nearer to being a

---

*Pali Canon: *Udana*, 8:3, quoted in Hans Kung et al., *Christianity and the World Religions*, trans. Peter Heinegg (Garden City, N. Y.: Doubleday, 1986), p. 301.

practicing Buddhist than he was to being a Catholic communicant, despite his declared veneration of the Virgin of Chartres.

The Sanskrit root *budh* has nothing to do with either "light," as propounded in Arnold's epic, or with "enlightenment." Nor does it suggest clarity as produced from external agencies. Buddha means literally "The Awakened One" or "The One Who Has Come to Understanding." A Buddhist is one who comprehends, but that in no way suggests an ultimate stasis of realization. Step by indicated step, by the practice of constant mindfulness, understanding arrives. The core of personality is not a "soul," as the Occident imagines, but the empirical, functioning self. On this path, he who aims at understanding attains freedom from the vanity of "I am" or "me." The whole of Buddhist method is a process toward purification of the given self. Certain personal, individual needs are admitted. There are legitimate and illicit needs. Buddhism is not nihilism, as adumbrated by Schopenhauer, but a diminishing of irrelevance. It is the destruction, orderly and logical, of obsessive hindrance. It leads toward Nirvana, which is neither negative nor inexpressible but rather a state free from diffusion and illusion. In these aspects it is positive, since it is directed at stability, liberty, truth, peace, purity, and security.

The Sanskrit root *nibbana* means "cool," implying transformation from hot (passion) to cold (equanimity). Nirvana is an object of knowledge or developed vision. It is desirable, external, like a work of art; internal, like some pleasant or valuable interior condition. It is attainable through a method and a discipline. When Buddha died, "His mind was firm, without exhalation or inhalation. When the Sage passed away, free from desire, having found peace, he endured pain with active mind: the liberation of the mind was [like] the extinction of a lit lamp."

The historic Sakyamuni (Sage of the Sakya class) pronounced: "The road of political wisdom is an unclean path of falseness." Adams would not have disagreed. When he was in Japan, he took scant notice of the Meiji revolt, then at high tide, which opened a sealed society to worldwide power play. Nor did he devote attention to ritual, liturgy, or the connection between Shinto nature-worship and Northern Buddhism derived from China. Conscious of the vast prestige that art had lent the western churches, he sought some contemporary equivalent in the eastern mode.

In the limitless Petals of the Lotus, Adams was drawn by entities explicit in sculpture, mute but visible, characterized yet passive, immediate but timeless, a lodged likeness unlike all else, mortal and immortal, recognized in its proximity yet ultimate and transcendent. He must have known Emerson's "Brahma," a poem memorized by every good Boston Brahmin:

If the red slayer think he slays,
> Or if the slain think he is slain,
They know not well the subtle ways
> I keep, and pass, and turn again.

Far or forgot to me is near;
> Shadow and sunlight are the same;
The vanished gods to me appear;
> And one to me are shame and fame.

They reckon ill who leave me out;
> When me they fly, I am the wings;
I am the doubter and the doubt,
> And I the hymn the Brahmin sings.

The strong gods pine for my abode,
> And pine in vain the sacred Seven;
But thou, meek lover of the good!
> Find me, and turn thy back on heaven.*

(On 21 December 1880, Clover wrote to her father: "A high old-fashioned snowstorm here; the attempts at sleighing numerous and humorous. 'If the red sleigher thinks he sleighs,' Ralph Waldo Emerson would point him to the Brighton Road for the genuine article.")


## XV.


ADAMS and La Farge embarked for the Orient on 12 June 1886, arriving 2 July. The Pacific Ocean had behaved at its worst, indulging in one of its most contrary storms: "We have been more miserable by the linear inch than ever two woebegone Pagans, searching for Nirvana, were before. . . . Four female missionaries [aboard ship] . . . sing and talk theology, two practices I abhor," wrote Adams.

Both men were well prepared with wide frames of reference when they arrived in Japan. Only too soon, they discovered there no supernal Nirvana but a retrograde, unhygienic domain. Food was of magniloquent nastiness. They managed to escape a bad outbreak of cholera with only slight infection. Along with Sturgis Bigelow, Ernest

---

*Emerson's poem is an almost literal translation of the Katha Upanishad, 2.19. See Robert Ernest Hume, *The Thirteen Principal Upanishads, Translated from the Sanskrit* (London: H. Milford, 1921).

Fenollosa became an insistent mentor. The son of a musician married to the daughter of a Salem East-India shipowner, he was born in Spain in 1853, the year Perry's "Black Ships" opened Japan to international trade. He converted from Catholicism to the Episcopal Church. A brilliant Harvard student, he was class poet of 1874. Four years later, he went to Tokyo and stayed. Though Adams and La Farge could not have been blessed with a more knowledgeable guide, Fenollosa would inevitably drive Adams into one of his less benevolent furies:

> He is a kind of St. Dominic and holds himself responsible for the dissemination of useless knowledge by others. My historical indifference to anything but facts, and my delight at studying what is hopelessly debased and degraded, shock his moral sense. . . . He has joined a Buddhist sect; I was myself a Buddhist when I left America, but he has converted me to Calvinism with leanings towards the Methodists.

Despite the assiduous ministrations of Fenollosa and more noble and scholarly guides, the irritations of primitive travel, an intractable language, and strange food, Adams was obliged to admit that the vision of Nikko was worth discomfort after all. Though Zen-oriented purists of the late twentieth century take a supercilious delight in downgrading the baroque splendor of Nikko's unbridled fantasy, it is one of the wonders of world architecture. The Tokugawa Shogunate of the seventeenth century, a relatively "decadent" military despotism, established in a dense forest of hundred-foot-tall cryptomeria spectacular congeries of lacquered and gilded pavilions, temples, and tombs reached by precipitate granite steps of exquisite carving and adornment. Adams learned that the tourist's phrase "See Naples and die" was an equivalent of "Never say *kekko* ['magnificent'] until you've seen Nikko." Leading to the realm of individual shrines and graves are miles of roads lined with six-hundred-year-old cedars, a required feudal taxation offered in semispiritual homage. Entering through the incredibly complicated bracketings of the Yomeimon Gate, traversing the coffered corridors leading to the solemn grandeur of Ieyasu's shrine, along walls and under ceilings encrusted with gold, past black-framed panels ablaze with chrysanthemum and poppy, phoenix and dragon, by pillars coruscating with angelic guardians, Adams photographed the twenty acres of glory erected by military monks in praise of Buddha Amida. He was greatly impressed:

> Japan is not the last word of humanity, and Japanese art has a well-developed genius for annoying my prejudices; but Nikko is, after all, one of the sights of the world. I am not sure where it stands in order of rank, but after the pyramids, Rome, Mme. Tussaud's wax-works, and 800 16th street [the Hay-Adams mansion], I am sure Nikko deserves a place. . . . When you reflect that the old Shoguns spent twelve to fourteen millions of dollars on this remote mountain valley, you can understand that Louis Quatorze and Versailles are not much of a show compared with Nikko.

80

Adams spent a thousand dollars for himself and another thousand for Hay on kake-monos, ceramics, drawings by Hokusai and Hiroshige, and kimonos for wives of friends that would launch a new vogue at Prides Crossing and Newport. For the glories of Nara and Kyoto he forgave a society he could not help despising. Warriors and the priests who raised them, a millennium gone, were buried as deep as those who had built Karnak. At Nikko, he complained to La Farge of "the deadening influence of Tokugawa rule, of its belittling of the classes whose energies were the true life of the country." A feudal military autocracy was responsible for tomb and temple. It was not passive priests but aggressive samurai who paid for the perfection of such grandeur. La Farge, with deeper insight, held any Egyptian parallel to be false, for Nikko, unlike Luxor or Denderah, was not built to defy time but to accept eternal peace. But La Farge was a Roman Catholic; his faith embodied Incarnation and Resurrection. He reminded Adams that the question most frequently asked in Boston was "Who am I?" whereas in Japan it was "What am I?" And Adams, to some degree, concurred: "Japan has the single advantage of being a lazy place. One feels no impulse to exert oneself; and the Buddhist contemplation of the infinite seems the only natural mode of life. Energy is a dream of raw youth."

In Nikko's fantastic dukedom of a glorious cemetery was one figure who regarded all human conflict with impersonal diffidence or, if one preferred, benevolence, although to many there was no certainty of either. Kan-non, Kwannon, Kuan-Yin, in China often male but in Japan more often female, bestowed mercy from a depthless fount, oblivious of time. Here time did not pass; it was an unbegun, unending constant through which men traveled in endless flux. Adams would come to a Nirvana of his own neither in Nikko nor in Nara, but at least he could indulge his wonderment on the carved and cast imagery of Kyoto and Kamakura in their ineffable residue. La Farge wrote sadly, "If only we had found Nirvana, but he was right who warned us [the reporter at Omaha] that we were late in the season of the world."

In Adams's overweening preoccupation with the Self, in his vanity and misery, however half-comprehended, the plasticity of local Buddhism held at least hints of deper-sonalized solace, that blessed annihilation that might be vouchsafed even one incapable or unworthy of belief. To him, the agnostic or Christian anarchist, Kan-non was graced with a woman's halo; from La Farge, something of a Mariolater, he could borrow parallels with the Mother of God, the Queen of Heaven, and also *Das Ewig-Weibliche*, Faust's Eternal-Feminine.

As for modern Japanese society, Adams had few good words. The women were "badly made and repulsive." Geishas, dancing, were "an exhibition of mechanical childishness" in which "the women's joints clacked audibly, and their voices were metal." His two main interests at home, politics and the pageant of the social world, held no interest for him here; local history was as closed a book as the language. He saved his praise for Japan's architecture even more than for its sculpture and painting. La Farge, constitutionally prone to a Pre-Raphaelite prettiness, executed with ease his genteel watercolors. Adams scolded, but later acknowledged with gratitude that his own serious attention had begun with La Farge's "analysis of the theme of [Japanese] architecture, and my feeling a sort of desire to rival him on a ground of fair competition. But I do not think I could grasp a subject in such clear and dispassionate mastery."

At Nikko, on the veranda of their dollhouse of paper screens and aromatic woodwork, near a thrillingly tall but often dry waterfall, Adams compared their life to a grown-up version of Tom Sawyer's and Huck Finn's. He read the *Paradiso*. Dante's Beatrice, the Blessed Virgin, merciful Kan-non were persistent essences realized by poets and artisans. These fueled his mind, corroborating more firmly his concept of some concrete memorial. Fenollosa drew him to the small nunnery of Chu-gu-ji, where there was a large sixth-century bronzed-wood image with "the face of a sweet loving spirit, pathetic and tender, with the eyes closed in inner contemplation. It dominates the whole room like an actual presence."

At the end of their stay, Adams and La Farge were at Kamakura paying their respects to the colossal Daibutsu. Borrowing a priest's camera, Adams photographed it. On their way back to Yokohama, Fuji-san was clouded in mist. On 2 October, they sailed for home. The two Americans might have agreed with Mrs. Bishop, the early lady-tourist author of *Unbeaten Tracks in Japan* (undated), who wrote that the country was "a study rather than a rapture, [but] its interest exceeded my largest expectations."

The three-week voyage home was relatively calm. Fenollosa was a shipboard companion, now free of the compulsions of a guide. Adams found leisure to survey the last months' experience in the easy exchange of La Farge's less demanding enthusiasm. On land at last, on 20 October, Adams wrote: "Japan and its art are only a sort of ante-chamber to China and . . . China is the only mystery left to penetrate. I have hence-forward a future. As soon as I get rid of [American] history, and the present, I mean to start for China, and stay there. In China I will find bronzes or break all the crockery."

To China he would never go. As for his trip to Japan, for all his finical remon-strances, crustiness, perversity, and disdain for the human conditions of Japanese life, one can nevertheless deduce that Adams had been profoundly moved. Mere discomfort on a mundane level would not mar his devotion to the changeless solicitude of Kan-non, which indirectly, through La Farge's impressions, would filter through to the studio of Augustus Saint-Gaudens.

# XVI.

As soon as his train had crossed the continent, Adams was summoned to Quincy to the deathbed of his father. One searches in vain to uncover any genuine sentiment toward a man who had been very fond of Henry the boy. Whatever his grief, he stayed silent, perhaps with an increased fortitude gained from the granite of the Tokugawa tombs. Yet it was he who was assigned to compose the epitaph of Charles Francis Adams:

> Trained from youth in politics and letters
> His manhood strengthened by the convictions
>     Which had inspired his fathers. . . .
> He failed in no task which his government imposed
>     Yet won the respect and confidence of two generations. . . .

Brooding on such a stiff encomium, Adams might have mused at how many of those words applied to himself. But whatever his anguishing limitations, self-knowledge as exculpation was not one of his failings. Never in any of his writings had he mentioned Clover as an individual. At last and at least he would admit, "I have not heard my wife's name spoken for twenty years. That was a great mistake." On his return to the half-empty house now completed on Lafayette Square, his thoughts must have turned ceaselessly to one no longer at his side. So far, Marian Hooper Adams had gained no fixed memorial. How many years ago had La Farge worked along with Saint-Gaudens on the scaffolding of Trinity Church, painting the saints Paul and James. Its architect was gone.

*Henry Adams*

The painter's suggestion for a sculptor, given the intimacy of long admiration, was almost inevitable. La Farge's part in the eventual monument can hardly be forgotten. In an interview published in the *Washington Evening Star* of 17 January 1910, he told of going to Saint-Gaudens's studio with Adams to propose the work. Knowing that the sculptor was busy with many projects, they sent no word that they were coming for fear he would then be prepared to decline such an arduous, challenging commission. As the interviewer recounted La Farge's recollections:

> Mr. Adams described to him in a general way what he wanted, going, however, into no details, and really giving him no distinct clew, save the explanation that he wished the figure to symbolize "the acceptance, intellectually, of the inevitable." Saint Gaudens immediately became interested, and made a gesture indicating the pose which Mr. Adams words had suggested to his mind. "No," said Mr. Adams, "the way you're doing that is a 'Penseroso.'"
>
> Thereupon the sculptor made several other gestures until one of them struck Mr. Adams as corresponding with his idea. As good luck would have it, he would not wait for a woman model to be brought in and posed in accordance with the gesture indicated by the sculptor, so Saint Gaudens grabbed the Italian boy who was mixing clay, put him in the pose and draped a blanket over him. That very blanket, it may be stated here, is on the statue, and forms the drapery of the figure.
>
> "Now that's done," said Mr. Adams. "The pose is settled. Go to La Farge about any original ideas of Kwannon. I don't want to see the statue until it's finished."

Perhaps now Adams recalled Richardson's curt response to his complaint that his house was less satisfactory than Hay's. In any case, Saint-Gaudens was extremely busy with a plethora of demanding jobs. Adams would try to prove himself a patient patron. On 29 April 1888, he wrote briefly in a journal—less a diary than a series of notes:

> At New York I saw La Farge and St Gaudens, and made another step in advance towards my Buddha grave. Nothing now remains but to begin work, and St Gaudens hopes to play with it as a pleasure while he labors over the coats and trousers of statesmen and warriors.
>
> Sunday, September 2 [1888, Washington]. Clarence King was here one day this week. Have reached Chap. II, Book V [of his history of the United States]. Contract made with Stanford White for stone-work of Buddha monument at Rock Creek. Have written to St Gaudens to send his contract for signature.
>
> Sunday, September 30 [1888]. . . . Steadily working towards my demise. . . . Have sold at a sacrifice of two thirds all the railroad stock I still own, and beginning to provide twenty thousand dollars for St Gaudens and Stanford White. The world steadily narrows towards a point two years distant.
>
> Sunday, 10 December [1888]. . . . On returning to New York I went yesterday to see St Gaudens who has begun the Buddha. We discussed the scale, and I came away telling him that I did not think it wise for me to see it again, in which he acquiesced.

At the start, the sculptor felt he had little enough of any end in view to prompt him, but quickly, on Adams's departure from his studio, jotted down: "Adams. Buddha. Mental repose. Calm reflection in contrast with violence or force in nature."

However much both Adams and La Farge may have considered the principles underlying the concept of the future memorial to be fixed, the sculptor privately held other ideas that were not similarly established. He made a series of preliminary studies in rough clay, then cast them in plaster with hooks in their plaques so that they could be hung up for study. Strangely, there was an absolute shift from any notion of Kan-non; the god-goddess of mercy was supplanted by Socrates. One sketch shows the traditional image of the bearded philosopher, holding in his right hand what seems to be the cup of hemlock. He is seated against something that suggests an Attic graveslab. Had this been found remotely satisfactory, the historic coincidence of self-slaughter would have been invoked. But Socrates was condemned by the state; Clover, by herself. And in spite of an early agreement that Adams was to stay away and not impinge upon the project, Saint-Gaudens could not forbear writing him:

Do you remember setting aside some photographs of Chinese statues, Buddha, etc., for me to take away from Washington? I forgot them. I should like to have them now. Is there any book *not long* that you think might assist me in grasping the situation? . . . I propose soon to talk with La Farge on the subject, although I dread it a little.

. . . If you catch me in, I will show you the result of Michelangelo, Buddha, and St. Gaudens. I think what I will do may not be quite as idiotic as if I had not had all these months to "chew the cud."

. . . The question now with me is, rock or no rock; which, when I have another sketch indicated, I will show La Farge. [Stanford] White holds that the rock requires a different treatment from the seat [opposite the figure], and to prove it has made a stunning scheme. I'm half inclined to give in to him, but that also La Farge must pass on.

If the figure is cast in bronze in several pieces it can be set up in Washington about July first. This I consider inadvisable, as the statue can be cast in virtually one piece which is seldom done in these days; for this, however, twelve weeks are necessary. Should this be decided on and you be away when the figure is cast, I propose to bronze the plaster cast and set it up at once in the place that the bronze will occupy in the monument in Washington, so that you can judge of its effect in metal. In any event, I should like to have you see the face of the figure in the clay. If it were not for that part of the work I would not trouble you. But the face is an instrument on which different strains can be played, and I may have struck a key in a direction quite different from your feeling in the matter. With a word from you I could strike another tone with as much interest and fervor as I have had in the present one.

My relations with you in this matter have been so unusually agreeable that you can appreciate how much I am troubled at the prospect of not having the bronze itself in place on July first.

85

That was not to be the last delay. Almost two years later, on 19 August 1890, Adams, bound for Honolulu and the South Seas, wrote a friend from the sleeping car Pocatello, then crossing the Plains of Laramie: "Should you pass through Washington next year, I wish you would drive out to Rock Creek Church, behind the Soldiers' Home, to see the grave...where I trust that a work will be finished which I must leave unseen."

He wrote home continually, begging for news of the memorial's stages of completion, soliciting his friends' frank opinions. From the following letter, it is clear that the sculptor was scrupulous to a fault in fulfilling the slightest nuance of Henry Adams's intention. Homer Saint-Gaudens often did not trouble to date his father's letters, but this was probably written some time in late 1888 or in 1889:

> I meant that my first communication to you should be a word asking you to come and see the figure. However I have to give that up. You asked that, in whatever was placed back of the figure, the architecture should have nothing to say, and above all that it should not be classic. White and I have mulled over this a great deal, with the enclosed results. I do not object to the architecture or its classicism as indicated in Number One [of sketches enclosed], whereas Number Two would, we both fear, be rather unpleasant. This matter must be settled immediately, and I cannot do that without asking you. I do not think the small classical cornice and base can affect the figure and, to my thinking, the monument would be better as a whole. [Adams chose this.]
>
> If, however, the plain stone at the back of Number One, marked "front," is much preferable to you, we will carry it out.
>
> In about ten days you will hear from me, asking you to run on. I've demolished the figure several times, and now it's all going at once.

Later:

> The monument is finished and all that remains to be done is the grading and the planting of some trees in the rear of the seat. White's work appears to me to be very fine, sober, and strong. As to my work, you must judge for yourself. The rock on which the figure is seated needs to be rubbed in order to get it darker. This will be done at once. I did not do it before setting up the work as I was uncertain as to the effect of the stone. That, however, is a small matter.

Homer Saint-Gaudens felt that his father was content with what he had finally accomplished. In 1903, the sculptor told his wife and his son that he wished he "could remodel that fold between the knees. It makes too strong a line," he said, but concluded, "I believe that would be all I would do."

On Sunday, 1 June 1891, Adams wrote from Papeete to Elizabeth Cameron:

> The Richmond suddenly arrived this morning, bringing your March and April letters from Samoa, with the photographs of St Gaudens' work. St Gaudens himself, and Dwight [Theodore Frelinghuysen Dwight, a young friend of Adams's who was staying

in the Washington house], and Hay also wrote about it, but none of them gave so much as you, though Hay's little description of it gave me a regular old-fashioned fit of tears, and I have not yet at all recovered from the effect of reading and re-reading what you have all said. As for you, I can say nothing that I have not said so often as to be ashamed of not saying more. I am infinitely grateful. You make me feel as though my last anxiety was removed, and I had no more to worry about in life. If the statue is half what you describe it, I can be quite contented to lie down under it, and sleep quietly with her. At the end of all philosophy, silence is the only true God.

Mrs. Cameron, in a letter of 14 March 1891, had written: "The figure is something more than life size, and the bronze is most beautiful in color. . . . The whole pose is strong and calm, full of repose. I was disposed to criticise a little the background of the figure, but I think no judgement would be fair until the grass, hedge, and general green background to it is all there. The stonework — the bench — is beautiful."

A day after receiving her letter and photographs she had enclosed, Adams wrote to Theodore Dwight:

I will not make up my mind from the photographs, whether I am entirely satisfied with the work. I cannot be quite sure of my own feeling until I see it. At any rate the photographs make certain that I shall not *dis*-like it, which is a vast comfort for me, who have dreaded hating it. Of course I cannot hope that my own thoughts passing through another man's mind and hands, will come out in a shape familiar to me; my only anxiety is to know that the execution is better than the ideal.

To John Hay, who had been most enthusiastic about the figure, Adams wrote from Fiji on 21 June 1891:

If it not exactly my ideal, it is at least not hostile. St Gaudens is not in the least oriental, and is not even familiar with oriental conceptions. Stanford White is still less so. Between them, the risk of going painfully wrong was great. Of course White was pretty sure to go most astray, and he has done so; but probably the mistakes are not so serious as to over-balance the merits. . . . I know of very few people whose judgement on such a work would carry much weight with me, so I am not greatly concerned about what is said or thought; but after having your approval, I am satisfied.

Nevertheless, Adams must have been mollified by an accumulating crescendo of praise from those in whom, for better or for worse, he had some trace of confidence. With a twitch of grace, he found himself capable of an approximation of gratitude to Saint-Gaudens, to whom he wrote on 23 June 1891 from Siwa, in the Fiji Isles:

As far as the photographs go, they are satisfactory, but I trust much more to the impression produced on John Hay, who writes me that he has been to Rock Creek to see the figure. "The work is indescribably noble and imposing. It is to my mind Saint-Gaudens's master-piece. It is full of poetry and suggestion, infinite wisdom, a past without beginning and a future without end, a repose after limitless experience, a peace to which nothing matters — all are embodied in this austere and beautiful face and form."

Certainly I could not have expressed my own wishes so exactly, and, if your work approaches Hay's description, you cannot fear criticism from me.

Originally, Saint-Gaudens was furious that photographs had been forwarded to Adams in Tahiti, robbing him of a first impression derived from facing the statue. Virtual precedents may have lain dormant in the mind of the sculptor since his years in Rome. Michelangelo's Sistine figures, individually, have almost become part of the race memory, and particularly meaningful for Saint-Gaudens was the Delphic Sybil, lips parted as if prophesying to the Gentiles the coming of Christ, or the mother of Jesse, her hand raised in a curious twisted gesture, drawing her seamless toga around her child.

Sometime afterward, as an elaborate joke, Saint-Gaudens modeled Adams's profile, attached to a winged porcupine's body, on a bronze medallion bearing a Latin inscription: "To the angelic porcupine Henry Adams." Whatever Adams's feelings and behavior on oppressive occasions may have been, one is grateful a century later that his quills, when loaded with ink, did have the grace of an angel. For his intelligence and charm he can be pardoned much. As for the memorial, it is best left to him to certify in his own words the residue of his own final judgment. In his *Education* is a sonorous recapitulation of his first actual encounter with Saint-Gaudens's masterpiece. A less known and more spontaneous version of it was contained in a letter to Elizabeth Cameron written on 19 April 1903:

> At dinner the other evening we were chaffing St. Gaudens because of his Rock Creek figure, which he has to tell the meaning of. As he never could use words at all, at least in explaining thoughts, he stumbles over it wearily. His wife, as usual, gets impatient, for she says now it is their favorite joke that whenever they go out to dinner here some one always drags St. Gaudens into a corner and says: "Do tell me what you meant in that figure?" As La Farge in his introspective way remarked, he might answer that the figure was meant to express whatever was in the mind of the spectator; but this would be too fine. To a wearily historical mind like mine, it is curious that what would have been elementary to every other age of mankind, and which any beggar of Benares or Tokio would read at a glance, is a sealed mystery to the American mind. As I sit there, and listen to the comments of the stream of visitors, I am astounded at the actually torpid perceptions of the average American; and the worst of all is the clerical preacher. He can see nothing but Despair. He shows what his own mind is full of; but the idea of Thought has been wholly effaced.

Adapting from this letter or reworking his copy, Adams expressed himself more formally and with increased emphasis in his book:

> Most took it for a portrait-statue, and the remnant were vacant-minded in the absence of a personal guide. None felt what would have been a nursery-instinct to a Hindu baby or

a Japanese jinricksha-runner. The only exceptions were the clergy, who taught a lesson even deeper. One after another brought companions there, and, apparently fascinated by their own reflection, broke out passionately against the expression they felt in the figure of despair, of atheism, of denial. Like the others, the priest saw only what he brought. Like all great artists, St. Gaudens held up the mirror and no more. The American layman had lost sight of ideals; the American priest had lost sight of faith. Both were more American than the old, half-witted soldiers who denounced the wasting, on a mean grave, of money which should have been given for drink.

With what eyes might Saint-Gaudens have viewed his finished labor? Adams complained that he stayed famously close-mouthed on the subject, as if words were admissions of ineptitude in the face of an art that should speak for itself:

> Of all the American artists who gave to American art whatever life it breathed in the seventies, St. Gaudens was perhaps the most sympathetic, but certainly the most inarticulate.... All the others — the [Richard Morris and William Morris] Hunts, Richardson, John La Farge, Stanford White were exuberant; only St. Gaudens could never discuss or dilate on an emotion, or suggest artistic arguments for giving to his work the forms that he felt.

But Adams was forced to admit: "He could not imitate, or give any form but his own to the creations of his hand. No one felt more strongly than he the strength of other men, but the idea they could affect him never stirred an image in his mind."

The sculptor, as professional craftsman, might have taken satisfaction at the advance over his earlier essays in mortuary art. In 1873, at the very start of his career, he was awarded a commission for a figure of *Silence*, to be set at the top of a flight of stairs in the Masonic Building at the corner of Sixth Avenue and Twenty-third Street in Manhattan. Now in a Masonic hospital in Utica, New York, *Silence* is a heavily draped female figure, the head clumsily wrapped, one long extended finger pressed against the lips. In all its niggling detail, *Silence* holds no anticipation of the heroic abstraction in Rock Creek; it even recalls the clutter of wan marble maidens that Clover so deplored in William Wetmore Story's Roman studio. Of the figure, Saint-Gaudens wrote, "The less said the better." He also had a contract for the tomb of Edward Morgan, a governor of New York state who had been influential in gaining for him the *Farragut* commission, which marked the launching of a great career. The Morgan tomb was an elaborate project, involving at first eight angelic figures, then reduced to five and committed only to clay and plaster models. The uncut marble was destroyed by fire, and the whole abandoned.

Riddles resident in the Adams bronze would increasingly rankle a multitude of questioning observers over the years to come, provoking angelic porcupine stabs of quirky prickings. Adams scolded President Theodore Roosevelt for silly comments:

89

"But!!! . . . should you allude to my bronze figure, will you try to do St. Gaudens the justice to remark that his expression was a little higher than sex can give. As he meant it, he wanted to exclude sex, and sink it in the idea of humanity. The figure is sexless."

Kan-non, Kwannon, Kuan-yin, however, was not sexless; he, she, it embodied both natures common to the species. Adams may have been pleased (to whatever degree) that he had caused to come into being a work of art that struck some common chord, no matter the level of response. The figure was greeted almost immediately as a lofty puzzle. Though Adams rarely cared to forward a hint as to a "meaning" or a title, in a letter of 14 October 1895 to Richard Watson Gilder, he admitted: "The whole meaning and feeling of the figure is in its universality and anonymity. My own name for it is 'The Peace of God.' La Farge would call it 'Kwannon.' Petrarch would say: 'Siccome eterna vita è veder Dio,' and a real artist would be very careful to give it no name that the public could turn into a limitation of its nature."

Mrs. Barrett Wendell, the wife of a much-loved Harvard professor of English literature, wrote Homer Saint-Gaudens with what would perhaps be the simplest explanation:

> On Thursday, May 5, 1904, I was in the Rock Creek Cemetery . . . when Mr. St.-Gaudens and Mr. John Hay entered the little enclosure. I was deeply impressed and asked Mr. St.-Gaudens what he called the figure. He hesitated and then said, "I call it the Mystery of the Hereafter." Then I said, "It is not happiness?" "No," he said, "it is beyond pain, and beyond joy." Mr. Hay turned to me and said, "Thank you for asking. I have always wished to know."

Given his nature, all interpretations and speculations failed in the end to placate Adams himself. To allow that would have been contrary to his porcupinal disposition. In 1902, he felt constrained to write Saint-Gaudens:

> Every now and then in certain lights, I see or think I see, an expression almost answering to defiance in the mouth and nostrils. You did not put it there nor did I.
>
> What puzzles me is whether the figure says this to me, or I say it to the figure . . . I shall never know. I have gone on reading and thinking . . . without ever finding an answer to the question which is the absolute, the ultimate, the universal: Infinity or Finity.

His hapless solipsism had always defeated his rationality. He could not bear the possibility that there was indeed a mystery past his potential reckoning. What there was could be, should be, must be known. Yet in his partial summation, one single word catches fire as if sparked from smoldering ash. DEFIANCE! Shy of forced utterance, Clover's ghost mocked reason. *Defiance?* Could this be tardy protest? Or, if mute accusation, was it his just due? Had he not striven tirelessly, passionately, in perfect

90

taste, to perpetuate the wick of her spirit so that it might glow with healing forbearance, however culpable or unworthy he himself might be deemed? It was now she, absolved of all need for apology or excuse, who loomed as legend, incarnate in cast metal. As far as his borrowed oriental criteria went, that was barely to be pardoned. The monument offered no affirmation of the unutterable; instead, it perpetuated Clover's frail humanity, which had transcended failure—hers, his, Saint-Gaudens's. Her timeless bronze, open to any interpretation yet exceeding every one, would personify consolation for many who would never know her name. Was it no small triumph for her that it was on her weak vessel of despair that Kan-non, Our Lady of Chartres—divinities Adams had hoped he could adore—had bestowed a peace that surpassed even his understanding?

Around New Year's Day 1877, Adams gave Clover a small copy of the Gospels in Greek and Latin, both of which were legible to her study. That was when they had first moved from Harvard and Boston to Washington and their horseback rides in Rock Creek Park. In the back of the Bible, she scribbled hints toward survival. Among them: *Fuge: Late: Tace* ("Flee: Endure: Be still"). And below:

> *Aux coeurs blessés*
> *l'ombre et le silence.*

# SELECT BIBLIOGRAPHY

Adams, Henry. *The Education of Henry Adams.* 1918. Reprint, with an introduction by D. W. Brogan. Boston: Houghton Mifflin, 1961.

——. *A Henry Adams Reader.* Edited and with an introduction by Elizabeth Stevenson. Garden City, N. Y.: Doubleday, 1958.

——. *Henry Adams and His Friends: A Collection of His Unpublished Letters.* Compiled and with an introduction by Harold Dean Cater. Boston: Houghton Mifflin, 1947.

——. *The Letters of Henry Adams.* Edited by Worthington Chauncey Ford. 2 vols. Boston: Houghton Mifflin, 1930; 1938.

Adams, James Truslow. *The Adams Family.* New York: Literary Guild, 1930.

Adams, Marian Hooper. *The Letters of Mrs. Henry Adams: 1865–1883.* Edited by Ward Thoron. Boston: Little, Brown and Company, 1936.

Brooks, Van Wyck. *Fenollosa and His Circle.* New York: G. P. Putnam's Sons, 1962.

Coomaraswamy, Ananda. *Buddha and the Gospel of Buddhism.* London: G. G. Harrap, 1928.

Dryfhout, John H. *The Work of Augustus Saint-Gaudens.* Hanover, N. H.: University Press of New England, 1982.

Fields, Rick. *How the Swans Came to the Lake: A Narrative History of Buddhism in America.* Boulder, Colo.: Shambhala, 1981; distributed by Random House, New York.

Friedrich, Otto. *Clover.* New York: Simon and Schuster, 1979.

Johansson, Rune E. A. *The Psychology of Nirvana.* London: George Allen and Unwin, 1969.

Kaledin, Eugenia. *The Education of Mrs. Henry Adams.* Philadelphia: Temple University Press, 1981.

Levenson, J. C., et al. *The Letters of Henry Adams.* 3 vols. Cambridge: Belknap Press of Harvard University Press, 1982–.

Samuels, Ernest. *Henry Adams: The Middle Years.* Cambridge: Belknap Press of Harvard University Press, 1958.

Scheyer, Ernst. *The Circle of Henry Adams.* Detroit: Wayne State University Press, 1970.

Unless otherwise designated, the photographs in the text are the work of Marian Hooper Adams and are reproduced in this book by Courtesy of the Massachusetts Historical Society. Exceptions are those on pp. 46, Courtesy of the Harvard University Archives, and 75, Courtesy of Henry La Farge, James L. Yarnall, and Mary A. La Farge, *Catalogue Raisonné of the Works of John La Farge*, 3 vols. (New Haven: Yale University Press, forthcoming).

Permissions to use the following extracts are acknowledged with gratitude: on p. 42, from Caroline Tappan's poem "Disenfranchised," by permission of the Houghton Library, Harvard University: on p. 55, from W. H. Auden, "The Virgin and the Dynamo," in *The Dyer's Hand and Other Essays*, by permission of Random House, Inc., copyrighted in 1950; on p. 77, from Hans Kung, Josef von Ess, Heinrich von Stietencron, and Heinz Beckert, *Christianity and the World Religions*, trans. by Peter Heinegg, by permission of Doubleday and William Collins Sons & Co., copyrighted in 1986. The passages from the correspondence of Henry Adams and Marian Hooper Adams quoted throughout the essay appear by Courtesy of the Massachusetts Historical Society.

*Published by*
*The Metropolitan Museum of Art, New York,*
*and distributed by*
*Harry N. Abrams, Inc., New York*

*John K. Howat, The Lawrence A. Fleischman Chairman*
*of the Departments of American Art*

*Mary-Alice Rogers, Editor, The William Cullen Bryant*
*Fellows Publications, The American Wing*

*Design, Typography, and Production Supervision*
*by Howard I. Gralla*

*Composed in Monotype Bell by Michael & Winifred Bixler*

*Printed by Meriden-Stinehour Press*

*Bound by Acme Bookbinding Company*